I0825955

INTENTIONAL INTIMACY

BECOMING ONE IN OUR HEAVENLY FATHER THROUGH

INTENTIONAL *Intimacy*

SANDI GLEE

Published by *in*HOPE Publishing

ISBN Number: 978-0-9567277-9-4

Cover Design and Interior Design Layout by:

Christopher Ballew
@thechrisballew

Printed in the United States of America

I dedicate this book to my three sons—Ashley Robert, Christopher Michael, and Nicolas Andrew. You gave me the greatest assignment of my life: to be your mother and raise you in the love of Jesus Christ. Because of you three, I have an understanding of selfless love and the importance of nurturing relationships. You are precious gifts from my Heavenly Father, and I cherish each of you; you fill my heart. Because of you, I have two beautiful daughters-in-love and four beautiful grand-babies who have expanded my heart, and my life is overflowing with the goodness of the Lord. They have brought me to a depth in love that I never knew existed. I am rich indeed and count it an honor and privilege to receive such beautiful promises from the Lord. All of you are my blessings.

Mothering you three boys came with many challenges and lessons along the way, but the entire journey has been a part of what has molded me into the woman of God I am today. I dedicate this book to you because you have always been my most significant source of inspiration to be my very best throughout years of process. I dedicate this book to you because you are now men who love the Lord with all of your heart, soul, and mind, and in that, I can see that I loved you right.

Contents

ACKNOWLEDGEMENTS

As I have finished writing my first book, I look back and see all the people God has put in my path to help me accomplish this labor of love. Through your prayers, steadfastness to walk with me, and financial love gifts, you have helped bring this book to fruition. Family and friends, acquaintances, and strangers have helped me see this work to the end. From conception to this book's birth, I have learned so much about myself, people, and relationships. The world of writing a book was new to me and challenged me to go beyond my own comfort zone at times to see this come to life. With the input, words of wisdom, help, and encouragement of so many, God has painted a beautiful picture of how we truly need each other as we go through the earth on this journey called life. Fort that I am eternally grateful.

ALL my thanks go to you, Abba Father, for this book being part of my purpose in Your Kingdom. Did I ever want to write a book or think I would? No. But Father, in Your Word, You say you have great plans for me, and this was one of them. Your ways are always perfect in my life, and I thank You for giving me the gift of communication to bring Your truth in the earth.

Next, I want to give a HUGE thank you to my Spiritual father, Wynne Goss. When you prophesied over me and told me I would write a book, it was total confirmation of a word the Lord had already dropped in my spirit during my alone time with Him. Thank you for being obedient to speak forth what God whispered to you concerning me. Thank you for always setting aside time to be the voice of a father in my life and help me see from Jesus' perspective. What a treasure and gift from Heavenly Father you are in my life since losing my precious father, who was also my mentor and Spiritual father.

Marla Jackson, you have been my "two" for 23 years of full-time ministry. Jesus sent the disciples out two by two, and over the years, we have experienced how important it is to have a two in your life of ministry. When one is down, the other is always ready to encourage and help you get back up. Thank you for your willingness to journey with me as I entered the unfamiliar territory of writing. Thank you for being the cheerleader and always interested in reading the next chapter. Thank you for giving your time to listen as I would talk through my thought process before putting thoughts to pen and paper. Thank you for the endless hours of discussions, planning, scheduling, and follow through with the assignments we believe God has sent us forth to accomplish. You are a blessing from the Lord, a beautiful and precious gift that is cherished.

Thank you, Sena Yates, for gifting your personal time and skill to edit the book. Thank you for the hours you spent reading and re-reading to make sure my grammar is correct, my spelling and punctuation are accurate, and for helping me lose the contractions! As you could see, I like those a lot. Thank you for teaching me about formal writing, you have opened up a whole new world to me, and I am excited about other books in my Spirit. You are a beautiful person inside and out who carries wonderful gifts of our Father; thank you again for sharing. Being connected with you is truly a God thing, and it happened in God's perfect timing as it was time for edits to begin.

Christopher Michael, I don't even know where to begin, but thank you for gifting your precious time to read and re-read AND push me to explain in more depth my thoughts. You frustrated me, but I accepted the challenge and knew that I wanted to be understood. You are my child who always asked, "Why?" and I can see now how much of a gift that actually is in your life. You challenge people to go deep within their own thoughts so they can understand their true heart posture, discovering the joy and freedom of saying what we really mean and mean what we are saying. Thank you for the word accountability. Thank you for the countless hours of formatting and designing the book's layout and cover to convey the message of intentional intimacy with the Father. Your creativity has kept me fresh and relevant. Thank you for hearing my heart and bringing me into the 21st century. You are a treasure to all who have the privilege of knowing you.

Melanie Ward, thank you for your time and talents of make-up and photography. Thank you for showing me that I can be relevant and not limited by my age to look fresh and beautiful. I even thank you for insisting that I lose the dark lip liner; you know that was such a hard thing for me to let go of! Thank you for your photography skills and talent that challenged me to go beyond what I thought I could do. You are a precious gift to all who know you, and I thank God for connecting us.

FOREWARD

The price of all great relationships is death to self.

God the Father and his son Adam became disconnected because Adam did not remain in the place of faith. He was unfaithful to the One he was meant to be faithful to and love with all his heart. Instead, he put his faith in the words of a Serpent who was none other than The Great Deceiver and Father of Lies.

If Adam had turned away from the desire to be unfaithful to Father at the point of temptation, then there would have been no need for Calvary. Loving the Father enough to deny himself would have kept him inside the Garden of Eden and in perfect relationship and fellowship with his Father. Sadly, Adam loved himself more than his Father, and the union and intimacy they enjoyed were utterly broken.

It was at this very moment we see the Father's kind of love in action. He did not pull away from Adam and Eve, abandoning them to the consequences of their actions. Nor did He tell everyone about how they had rejected him. Instead, He immediately covered Adam and Eve's nakedness and shame, announcing His plan of redemption and reconciliation by His Son, the Seed (Genesis 3:15).

The Seed—Jesus Christ, The Son of God, The 2nd Adam—hung upon a cross between heaven and earth, between a heavenly Father and earthly sinful son, pouring out His perfect blood and life in order to reconcile the two parties. Because of His selfless love, the two became one again. This one act reveals the very heart of Jesus. He took the place of Adam and received the punishment for Adam's unfaithfulness. He paid the huge price which Adam could never pay for his mistake and did whatever it took to bring reconciliation to Father and son.

It required His blood and life. He gave up the right to be seen as innocent and instead, took the place of the guilty in order for the guilty party to be seen as the innocent party. He gave everything He had to give to make their relationship right and to keep it right forever. Such was the complete work of reconciliation by Jesus, that Paul states;

> *"For I am persuaded, that neither death, nor life, nor angels, nor principalities, nor powers, nor things present, nor things to come, Nor height, nor depth, nor any other creature, shall be able to separate us from the love of God, which is in Christ Jesus our Lord. (Romans 8:38-39 KJV)*

What Jesus joins together, let no one tear apart!

Surely, we see the work of all ministry is to bring reconciliation between Father and His lost 'sons,' between all the 'sons,' and to ***keep*** the unity between them all. Yet, the Body of Christ is more divided now than it has ever been in 2000 years. Why? Disunity and the breakdown of our relationships are evidence of our unwillingness to lay down our lives to love someone the way Jesus loves us - eternally, unconditionally, extravagantly, not depending on our perfect response. Jesus came and found us, paid the price for our sin, redeemed us, and reconciled us to Father. He did it all before we even realised we were in the wrong. Jesus didn't wait for us to find Him and do everything to put right all our wrongs. He now asks us to love others this same way, if at all possible.

The way we reveal our love to one another is the way we love our Father. If we unconditionally love the One we can't see, we will unconditionally love the one we can see. Our measure of loving His 'sons'—the Body of Christ—is the true measure with which we love Him.

The Kingdom of God is Relationships

> *"A new commandment I give to you, that you love one another; as I have loved you, that you also love one another. By this all will know that you are My disciples, if you have love for one another." (John 13:34-35 NKJV)*

If Jesus had just made the statement "A new commandment I give to you, that you love one another' we would be free to simply love others in any way we think love is expressed. But He didn't. He did not leave what He meant open to personal interpretation. By continuing to say, 'as I have loved you, that you love one another,' Jesus is declaring this is not open for discussion, private interpretation, theological discussion, or personal feelings. His words are clear, simple, and blunt. Love them as I have loved you.

Father gave the greatest gift He could give to save Adam and be reconciled with Him - the gift of His only Son (John 3:16).

Jesus gave the greatest gift He could give to save Adam and reconcile him to Father - His own life at Calvary.

Every born again believer is forgiven of all sin, saved, restored, their former life eradicated from Fathers memory and the life and nature of Jesus given to them, all because Jesus loved the Father and the son. He revealed what God's kind of love looks like; it is 'self'-sacrificial.

Therefore, God's kind of love is to be evidenced by His sons and daughters doing likewise to have and keep relationships. He even gave us the Spirit of Jesus to enable us to do what we say is impossible to do—to forgive and love the way He does. We have the Spirit that enables us to love the unlovely, forgive the unforgivable, take the blame when we are innocent and love His enemies, just as He did for us personally. His kind of love is so persistent it turns His enemies into His friends by the time He has finished with them.

As you hold the first pages of this book open and are ready to take this journey to read, I want to ask you three really serious questions.

Are you ready? Are you open? Are you willing?

Throughout this wonderful book, Sandi will hold your hand and take you on a step-by-step journey that will make you face some giants who have controlled your life for far too long. As Sandi navigates this journey, you will visit places that will make you face some things you've never faced before in order to help you live out the rest of your life, experiencing Father's love like never before.

Around every corner, you will be faced with truth; uncompromising truth, in-your-face truth, shocking truth. Yet, said with as much love and tact as possible to help you break free of stinking thinking and generational misunderstanding of God's Word, which we often hold onto.

This book is about relationships from the beginning to the end. Sandi invites us all to look candidly at our relationships with Father, ourselves, and one another. With no holds barred, she clearly shows the things that hinder us from obtaining a genuine depth of reality and love in relationships. I learnt a long time ago that the price for all great relationships is death to self. That is why I asked if you are ready, open, and willing. Are you?

I highly recommend Sandi, her ministry, and her book to you today.

Dr. Wynne Goss

Wynne Goss Ministries

Chapter 1

RELATIONSHIPS UNDER FIRE

Relationships are under attack; all relationships! And they're under attack because the enemy is trying to stop us from living the life that God desires for us—to be whole and well in spirit, soul, and body while simultaneously existing in loving relationships with Him and one another. If the enemy succeeds, we will simply go through a series of religious rituals because we are Christians, our lives completely void of purpose, power, or prosperity. Our relationship with God is the relationship the enemy fears the most, and his main objective is to destroy it. He relentlessly targets our relationship in The Church; relationships between husband and wife, parents and children, siblings, friends and society; and our relationship to food and health, money and material things, hoping that we will become so discouraged and disappointed that we stop trusting in our Heavenly Father, curse Him and walk away.

A relationship *in* God is a love relationship *with* God the Father, God the Son, and God the Holy Spirit. All three, yet one, want us to know who He is, how He feels toward us, who He is to others through us, and where He's headed. An intimate relationship with God is the only way to truly understand His love and His desire for us to prosper in all things and be healthy in every area of our life.

> *3 John 1:2 "Beloved, I pray that you may prosper in all things and be in health, just as your soul prospers."*

Our calling, purpose, and destiny depend upon our believing and trusting in God's love and care for us through a personal relationship with Him. The Body of Christ is under attack, and the enemy aims to destroy love and unity among all the members. The enemy is attacking us individually and corporately, hoping to dismantle the powerful force of The Church. WE ARE THE CHURCH! We don't *do* church or go to church. *We are The church* as we are *in a relationship* with Father God and each other.

As we *do* life, reality has a way of sucker-punching us at times, and our spirit cries out for God's mercy and grace to deliver and sustain us. When we cry out to Abba Father for His grace and mercy, what He hears is, "Bring me into *Your* realm of perfected love and freedom that makes me whole."

The enemy is well aware of God's desire for each of us to prosper in all things, be in health, and live in total peace with Him and others. Remember, he was an angel in Heaven *before* he was the snake in the garden. That means, before he was cast out of Heaven, he knew God's heart and had a relationship with Him. Now he walks about like a lion, seeking those whom he can devour.

> *1Peter 5:8 "Be sober, be vigilant; because your adversary the devil walks about like a roaring lion, seeking whom he may devour."*

The enemy comes to steal, kill, and destroy all that God has for us *in Him*. His strategy is to separate, isolate, and divide us—first from Father God, then from people—so we won't fulfill God's desire of a family in HIS Kingdom, making us weak.

God's design for all of us is to become *one flesh* with Him and *one body* with each other, a body filled with the love and power of Holy Spirit, which brings deliverance to the earth. The Word of God says the glory of the Lord will cover the earth, and guess what! That's the picture of UNITY—you and me, allowing God to come forth from our Spirit and pour Himself out on this earth.

Yes, the glory of God will cover the earth as we allow Him to live through our words, deeds, thoughts, and actions. Our interacting with each other and responding in love to one another is of highest priority to God, and He is looking to see where unity abounds because that's where He commands His blessing on us—life forevermore!

> *Psalm 133 "Behold, how good and how pleasant it is for brethren to dwell together in unity! It is like the precious oil upon the head, running down on the beard, the beard of Aaron, running down on the edge of his garments. It is like the dew of Hermon, descending upon the mountains of Zion; For **there** the Lord commanded the blessing—Life forevermore."*

WE ARE SPIRIT

Too many Christians are spiritually weak and immature because they have no understanding of who they are in Christ. The last part of 1 John 4:17 says, *"as He (Jesus Christ) is so are we in this world now."* Genesis 1:26 reads, *"Then God said, 'Let Us make man in Our image, according to Our* ***likeness****;....'"* According to this scripture, because God is spirit, and we must not forget that we are created first spirit, then soul and body. Our spirit will live for eternity, not our earth suits. Romans 8:10 says, *"And if Christ is in you, the body is dead because of sin, but the Spirit is life because of righteousness."* The same Spirit of God that walked the earth through Jesus Christ is the same Spirit that lives in us. So we are to be a healing, delivering, miracle-working power of God's love on this earth, and that power is spiritual. The enemy wants to get us focused on earthly matters that will die away.

A relationship in God
is a love relationship
with God the Father,
God the Son, and God
the Holy Spirit.

He attempts to kill us spiritually, or at the very least, make us weak and stunt our growth spiritually, so that we will always struggle to understand who we truly are and the *SUPER* part of our nature.

The Body of Christ is filled with Christians who are tired, sick, and weary of the calling, which we all accept in Christ—to love the Lord with all of our heart, soul, and mind and love each other as ourselves.

> *Matthew 22:37-39 "Jesus said to him, "'You shall love the Lord your God with all your heart, with all your soul, and with all your mind.' This is the first and great commandment. And the second is like it: 'You shall love your neighbor as yourself.'"*

Many in the Body of Christ simply cannot love with their whole heart and have become so discouraged, causing them to stagnate in their growth and understanding of how magnificent and powerful they are in Christ.

One of the oldest and most effective strategies of the enemy is to imprison God's people in bondage to the man-made system we have called the church, whose focus is on *doing* rather than *being*. And by the way, the church system will die away; it will not live eternally. But God's Kingdom will live for eternity!

If you were raised in the man-made system of church as I was, you know that there is a time to learn all the *dos* and *don'ts* of the Christian life according to the set of instructions and practices laid out by each denomination's system. I don't recall hearing much teaching on the love relationship with Father God and *receiving* His love and presence. I sang, "Jesus loves me this, I know," and even grew up knowing that God loved me, all without understanding the importance of my own relationship with Him.

The importance of relationship is to be modeled by *The Church*—the Body of Christ and NOT the world! Father's Kingdom model for His Church is seen through the anointing of apostle, prophet, evangelist, pastor, and teacher flowing together as one. (I'll talk about this more in Chapter 4). Suppose the enemy can keep us focused on the qualifications for membership and service within the system. In that case, he knows that our priority will become the system rather than the relationship with Father God, which is the thing that brings us all together as *ONE body*. The enemy's attractions and distractions are attacks designed to separate us from a spiritual relationship and desensitize us to the righteous truth of God's plan for us, which is to live *from* His Kingdom that is within each of us while being alive as *one body* through the marriage covenant with Christ.

> *Luke 17:20 "....The kingdom of God does not come with observation; nor will they say, 'See here!' or 'See there!' For indeed, the Kingdom of God* ***is within you****."*

> *Romans 7:4 "Therefore, my brethren, you also have become dead to the law through the body of Christ, that* ***you may be married to another****—to Him who was raised from the dead, that we should bear fruit to God."*

When a Christian begins to accept the world's views and opinions about our lives and others, we walk a very fine line of risk that can lead us straight to the broken relationships that so many are experiencing now. The Bible is clear that we are in the world but not of the world. The only way to live a full life in this world is to be a Christian who is in a loving, intimate relationship with Father God through Jesus Christ and trusting Him more than we trust ourselves. God desires that we allow ourselves to be discipled by Christ through a relationship rather than disciplined by the church system through a set of instructions and practices. The more we nurture our relationship with Daddy God in His love, the more we begin to hear Holy Spirit as He leads, guides, and directs us the same way He moved through Jesus.

THE ATTACK ON THE CHURCH

I know that I risk being ridiculed and called rebellious by many leaders when I talk in this manner. Still, the truth is The Church is responsible for the downfall of healthy, loving relationships across the globe because that is not what has been modeled from the pulpit. For the most part, the system has not encouraged or, in some cases, even allowed all the gifts of God's Spirit to flow together in unity, denying us the opportunity to glean from one another and grow together. We have not been taught or discipled to know that when we have received the perfect love of God the Father, God the Son, and God the Holy Spirit, then we have *all* we need to (1) be who God says we are, and (2) the ability to move in the gifts which He has given each of us through His unfailing love.

As a whole, the Body of Christ has spent more time emphasizing that our involvement and service within the church system is the most important element of a Christian's life. We have criticized and judged people harshly for issues as small as their attendance, tithing records, and volunteerism more than we have helped cultivate and encourage a healthy relationship that is personal between them and God.

True, these things are important and serve a purpose in the Believer's life, but they are not the *most* important and certainly not the things to be focused on in our leading. There are far too many leaders who are trying to be the Holy Spirit and police the behavior of God's people. Too many have established a modern-day ten commandments, penned from their own opinion and conviction, dictated from pulpits worldwide.

If we are in bondage to the man-made system of church it is difficult to accept the understanding that God's unfailing love is enough and is everything we need in our life. It is a challenge to accept all of who we are without the understanding that we don't do anything except receive perfect love from Father God. Most people live in fear of not doing enough for God so that He is pleased with them and accepts them as His own. They have believed the lie that *they could* do enough to make God accept them, and the man-made system has undergirded this lie with teaching and preaching that our behavior and works determine our eternal life with God.

> *1John 4:18-19 "There is no fear in love; but perfect love casts out fear, because fear involves torment. But he who fears has not been made perfect in love. We love Him because He first loved us."*

Perfect love—the love of God the Father—casts out fear of failure, conquers all obstacles, overcomes all insecurities, and becomes all we are to be for His Kingdom, not the church system. His perfect love will transform us, but we must be willing to humble ourselves and receive His perfect love in our imperfect condition.

Many Christians don't have real relationships with each other but are good at maintaining *"religious"* relationships. You know, the ones that exist because we see each other at Sunday and mid-week services. The ones where we hug and say, "It's so nice to see you." And "I've been praying for you." When, in reality, we haven't given them one thought throughout the week. The enemy has managed to desensitize us to the responsibility that we have concerning one another because we are a family, not just acquaintances in God's Kingdom. If we lose sight of *family*, then we WILL NOT KNOW THE KINGDOM OF GOD.

But, there is a revival of God's perfected love sweeping through the Body of Christ that brings reformation to individuals—the true Church—and He is changing how we relate to each other.

THE ATTACK ON MARRIAGE

The marriage covenant is the holiest covenant of God on the earth—the covenant of perfected love. Our relationship with Christ is likened to a marriage, as seen in Ephesians 5:25:

> *"Husbands, love your wives, just as* ***Christ also loved the church and gave Himself for her****, that He might sanctify and cleanse her with the washing of water by the word, that He might present her to Himself a glorious church, not having spot or wrinkle or any such thing, but that she should be holy and without blemish."*

God loves the whole and sent Jesus Christ to pay the ultimate price of redemption for the whole. The only way the whole will be one is when we allow the transformation by Holy Spirit in us on an individual basis. We receive this gift of life as individuals and come into a personal relationship with God the Father, Jesus His Son, and His precious Spirit ~ the Holy Spirit.

The enemy knows this and is forever trying to get us further and further away from that TRUTH manifesting in our reality. Too many Christians, especially this generation, have a perverted understanding of the relationship between a husband and wife and the true meaning of the marriage covenant ~ of becoming one flesh ~ and believe it is disposable. Many think they will try it, and if they don't like it, they will divorce and try with someone else. Perhaps, they never choose to marry but instead live a life together as though they were. Friends, that way of thinking is an opened door and invitation to the spirit of lust (lust of the flesh) to come right in and steal the truth of WHO love IS and who HE (JESUS) lives for.

Too many are guilty of looking to the world to understand marriage. The result is a big blown out event, emphasizing the event venue, party/reception, the wedding gown, tuxes, rings, exotic bachelor/bachelorette parties, and the honeymoon. I was actually with a bride as she was looking at venues for her wedding when the wedding planner asked her about the time frame for the ceremony and reception to the end of the night. Her response startled me because she is a young, beautiful Christian woman who said, "The ceremony will be fast because no one is really coming for that; they are all coming for the party afterward."

And true to her words, that's exactly what the attitude was for the entire evening. It was hard to even sense the Spirit of the Lord that night, and sadly now, she is divorced.

But, there is a revival of God's perfected love sweeping through the Body of Christ, and He is bringing us into the truth of what it means to be joined to Him and become one flesh with Christ. When we truly understand that *being one flesh* begins with *"Christ and me,"* then the dynamic to become one flesh

The answer is and has always been the same - JESUS!

with our bride or groom is supernatural. (God's *super* is put on our *natural!*)

THE ATTACK ON FAMILY

One of the saddest things to witness in this 21st century is the rampant blatant disregard for authority worldwide. There are far too many Christians who have allowed the disrespect, stubbornness, and disobedience of a child to rule and establish the house's temperature. The door has been opened wide to the spirit of rebellion, which will *ALWAYS* mature into witchcraft, manifesting as manipulation, scheming, and plotting to get their way. Look what the Word of God says about rebellion and stubbornness in 1Samuel 15:23 *"For rebellion is as the sin of witchcraft, And stubbornness is as iniquity and idolatry...."*

Too many parents today have the attitude that their life is theirs and rarely take the time to give themselves to their children through unconditional love. Sometimes love is expressed through discipling and disciplining them to bring forth a healthy, well-balanced, and whole adult. Parenting has been substituted with buying and giving children material things or sitting them down in front of the tv where they won't demand the parent's time and attention. Selfishness is replacing selflessness in parenting in this 21st century, and our children are suffering needless pain because of it. The next generation of adults won't understand sacrifice or obedience for love's sake if we don't begin to show true love to our kids now by giving ourselves to them through time and effort. Parents are allowing their child to practice witchcraft and idolatry by not engaging with them, ignoring them, and not dealing with their rebellion and stubbornness. This kind of dismissive behavior will always evolve into the parents being sucked into the "being at their wit's end" abyss. The child begins to idolize the power of their own manipulating, plotting, and scheming to get what they want, and parents are worn down to the point that they give the child control of the atmosphere in the home and daily life.

As parents, it is our responsibility to our kids to model the unconditional love of Abba Father, and sometimes that means standing with them and walking with them through the consequences of bad choices that they have made. Through God's perfected love in us, they will know that they are not alone to face their trials and tests of life, but love is journeying *with them*. Sadly, too many parents have taken the opposite approach and made statements like, "You made your bed; now lie in it!" Too many have left their children feeling abandoned during some of the hardest times of their lives, and they are growing up in an atmosphere that is highly saturated with deception and lies from the enemy being whispered to them.

But there is a revival of God's perfected love sweeping through the Body of Christ, and He is changing the way we love and respect one another. Our kids are being rescued from their hurt and pain. They are being restored to a beautiful place of knowing love that responds in obedience and respect for the giver of life.

THE ATTACK ON HEALTH

Many are sick and diseased because of a perverted relationship with food. Gluttony has become the norm for too many Christians today, eating just to be social and eating for comfort. We have replaced *eating to live* with *living to eat,* and it's killing us. Too many are filling their stomachs with two or three meals of rich or processed foods. They then exhibit no discipline to exercise and work off the extra calories, ultimately giving themselves to obesity and sickness. We turn to diets, pills, and other extreme measures to take the weight off because we haven't matured in the Spirit enough to discipline our flesh and move in self-control. Galatians 5:22 & 23 says, *"But the fruit of the Spirit is love, joy, peace, longsuffering, kindness, goodness, faithfulness, gentleness,* ***self-control.****"* Individuals are searching for a *quick fix* or the next fad diet instead of eating the fruit of self-control.

Because most Christians were taught in the church system not to drink, smoke, cuss, chew or go with those who do, we've been left with eating. I say this in jest, but many Christians are indeed sick now with heart disease, diabetes, arthritis, cancers, and countless other ailments because of an undisciplined lifestyle that has opened the door and allowed the spirit of infirmity to come in. Many have even made a place for that spirit to dwell by accepting the sickness and disease in their body as a cross they must bear. This kind of thinking has all been brought on by not understanding who we are in Christ. We are more than conquerors and able to overcome our fleshly desires. We fail when we refuse to draw from the power of Holy Spirit and exercise the fruit of self-control.

But, there is a revival of God's perfected love sweeping through the Body of Christ, and Holy Spirit is bringing life and strength to His people who allow Him to lead us into a life of discipline and power over our fleshly appetite.

THE ATTACK ON FINANCES

Many Christians have a perverted relationship with money and material things. Because they had very little as a child or didn't live a life of privilege and/or acceptance, many have made it a priority to have more, do more, and go more. They are trying to recreate the life which they didn't have to fulfill their desires. Let me remind us that money is only a tool to be used on this earth; we won't take it with us when we die!

Jesus even warns us about *serving* the spirit of mammon in Matthew 6:24, *"No one can serve two masters; for either he will hate the one and love the other, or else he will be loyal to the one and despise the other. You cannot serve God and mammon."* The word mammon originates from the Aramaic word *mammonas*, which means *confidence, i.e., wealth, personified; riches where it is personified and opposed to God.* The spirit of mammon causes one to have their confidence in wealth and possessions, and our

Heavenly Father wants us to have all confidence in Him. Money is simply a tool, but the spirit we choose to serve concerning the money is the issue to be considered in our lives. If money and material things are symbols of success and identity to us, then the door has been opened for the spirit of mammon to enter and dwell. Many are already suffering and may be in financial debt. And though they have much, they find themselves at a place of emptiness deep within themselves, usually too deep to see, and they need the healing hand of God to bring them out.

But there is a revival of God's precious Spirit sweeping through the Body of Christ bringing forth the truth that with God, we have an abundance of all good things in and through Him. According to the riches of Heaven, God provides for us. Philippians 4:19 *"And my God shall supply all your need according to His riches in glory by Christ Jesus."*

THE ATTACK ON IDENTITY

Too many have given themselves to a vicious cycle of trying to have the most, be the best and be the most popular, etc. in hopes of having their identity validated by others. Thus, the bondage to social media which enables a person to portray an *image* hiding the truth of emptiness and broken fragments in their life, which can be felt when we don't understand who we are in Christ. The enemy has capitalized on social media's advantage to keep the self-doubting, insecure, and rejected in a social web of deception. Too many people trust others' opinions through likes, comments, favs, upvotes, shares, and dislikes more than they believe and trust what God has to say about them.

But, there is a revival of God's perfected love sweeping through the Body of Christ, and through His healing power of love, He is changing the way we accept the truth of who we are in Christ.

TAKE RESPONSIBILITY

We who are spiritual leaders have a responsibility to direct, point, and guide everyone to the heart of the Father and forget the system for a minute. We are to nurture and love the family of God, not just a congregation but as extensions of God to us through His family. Healing and wholeness don't happen because of the system; healing and wholeness happen because of the unfailing perfect love of the ONE who is more than just God...He is our Father in Heaven, calling us into a relationship with Him.

The enemy will continue to roam around looking for those who aren't strong in the Lord because they don't live in a loving, nurtured relationship with the Heavenly Father, nor do they interact with Him. The answer is and has always been the same - JESUS! We find our completeness and full life in Him. The questions which we need to ask ourselves and as leaders encourage others to ask are:

Do I want to be drawn by the Father's love into His plan for my life and be one flesh with Jesus Christ to live a life of honor and privilege as a son or daughter of God?

Do I want to be healthy, whole, and prosper in all things?

Do I desire to be identified as Jesus with skin on?

Do I trust God for my life more than I trust myself?

Do I deny myself—what I think I know and who I think I am—and yield to God's ever-present love, allowing His Kingdom to come alive in me as His love transforms me?

As I reflect on all the relationships in my life and give my ear to listen to Holy Spirit, I can hear Him say He has brought reconciliation and correct alignment of all things according to His Word through His love. It is my responsibility to my own growth and maturity in Him to receive His love, which is the revival sweeping the land now. I must not take a passive posture, but I must engage and allow change to begin in me. I encourage you, the reader, to do the same.

Chapter 2

PERFECTED LOVE

Love can be very confusing. Does it exist in my heart and soul? Is it an emotion or a feeling? Do people fall in and out of love? Where does love begin? We've all probably had these questions and more concerning love at some point in time. For a Believer, we must go to the Word of God for our answer and gain understanding from Holy Spirit so that we are securely grounded on truth and the sure foundation of His Word. The definition of love is three words and found in 1John 4:7-8, and it says, *"Beloved, let us love one another, for love is of God; and everyone who loves is born of God and knows God. He who does not love does not know God, for* ***God is love.****"*

God is love ~ perfect love, and to know God is to know love. To know love is to know God. Love is spiritual because God is Spirit. *"God is Spirit, and those who worship Him must worship in spirit and truth."* ~ John 4:24.

To believe that love is an emotion or a matter of the heart is the same as saying it is natural and proves that we haven't received God's perfected love who is Spirit. Our understanding of love has often been defined through our emotions, thoughts, and will, which is our soul. God is drawing all of us into His realm of perfection according to His love for us. For many Christians, somehow, the truth of their spirit nature has been buried beneath a warped reality of circumstance and life situations, leaving them fighting in the natural to find solace and understanding in the midst of life chaos. The effort to discover and understand who they are in God hasn't been through divine revelation of Holy Spirit Himself but through personal thoughts, will and emotions. They're already headed down a dark and densely fogged path if *they* try and discover or invent what love is and who they are according to their mind.

God wants us to lean into Him and allow Him to bring us into His design and desire for us. He wants us to relax, relent, and fall into His arms and have an undeniable trust in Him and His love for us. To fully understand, receive, and become the perfected love of God, we must be willing to trust Him who created us and knew us before He even formed us in the womb. *"Before I formed you in the womb I knew you…."* ~ Jeremiah 1:5.

If we yield and trust Abba Father, His perfect love will spiritually transcend our thinking, knowledge, and understanding. It will transcend our emotions, feelings, and our self-will. The moment that we disarm our defenses and yield to Him and believe His Word is the moment we begin to receive His love. Love is spiritual and has the power to overcome our flesh, bringing us to spiritual wholeness. 1 John 4:17 says, *"Love has been perfected among us in this: that we may have boldness in the day of judgment; because* ***as He is, so are we*** *in this world."*

Love is the foundation of relationship and the reconciliation of all things back to Father God through Jesus Christ; it is supernatural. As I said previously, it doesn't come from any other source than God Himself. Love is birthed from the Spirit of God; it's not *natural* but *SUPER in nature*. Love is one of the mysteries of God that has been given to us to steward, *"Let a man so consider us, as servants of Christ and stewards of the mysteries of God."* ~ 1Corinthians 4:1, but how can we steward something that we have never experienced or have a wrong understanding of? God is love, *"He who does not love does not know God, for* ***God is love****."* ~ 1John 4:8, and His desire is that His people will come into His awareness and His consciousness so that our perception and perspective of who we are is a mirror of His perception and perspective. He desires that we experience His love so that we become love. As we *are* love like Jesus is, we are stewarding the very Spirit of God.

Love, in its truest form, cannot be explained but only experienced. The mystery of love is that it can only be *received* by us so that we *become* love. Many of us have believed that to get love, we must give love, and to give love, we must get love. But, the truth is that in Christ, we are love. The struggle isn't in the giving; the struggle is in the receiving. We cannot control how much love is given; we can only control how much love we receive. We struggle to receive love when we look outward and evaluate our own worth, judging ourselves against the standards we have accepted in our own thinking (some being false) and some that have been set in our foundation from early childhood.

Many suffer today in understanding self-worth and value because of mental, emotional, and/or physical abuse and misuse by others. For many, the fear of rejection and abandonment keeps them paralyzed in their minds, as well as physically, from

Love, in its truest form,
cannot be explained but
only experienced.

ever moving beyond the words, accusations, and fears with which the enemy has bombarded their thinking. Listen, if we do not allow love to transform our thinking and set healthy boundaries in our minds, then the enemy *WILL!* And his way always leads to dysfunction, disillusion, disappointment, and destruction in ourselves.

When we receive God, we receive love - unconditional and perfected love because God *is* love. We receive His love when we accept the truth that God sent his only son, Jesus Christ, to die for our sinful nature, and we give our lives and hearts to Him. In our state of unworthiness, God made a way for us to be reunited with Him. When we can grasp the truth of how much God loves us and how He showed it by sending Jesus, His most precious son, to die for us, we can be transformed and grow to love ourselves, then and only then can we become love to others.

To experience God's love, we must begin to see ourselves from God's perspective and not from our own. God sees us through eyes of love; we see ourselves through eyes filtered by our reality and circumstance. Through these fractured lenses, tinted by our dark sin nature, we judge ourselves to be either worthy or worthless. But the Word of God says that even what we think is righteous or worthy in and of ourselves is as filthy rags to God, *"But we are all like an unclean thing, and all our righteousnesses are like filthy rags; We all fade as a leaf, and our iniquities, like the wind, have taken us away."* ~ Isaiah 64:6.

Only the shed blood of Jesus that cleanses our lives will bring us into the redemptive love of God, making it possible to receive His love. When we catch a glimpse of God's love for us, even knowing our sin nature, we see that He spared nothing to save us. When we receive God's love and allow Him to redeem us, we become love, and it is impossible to control our *being* love. We *simply are!* God is moving in revival through His love now to bring all of His kids into the truth of *who He is in us*. The revelation of who He is can alter and change our very opinion of who we are, why we exist, and where we are headed. God's love is perfect and being perfected (the more we move away from our own way and thinking and closer to Jesus' ways and His thoughts) in us so that we become the power that will cast out all fear in our own life and overcome all the obstacles that have kept us from moving forward in God's desire for our life. 1 John 4:18 says, *"There is no fear in love; but perfect love casts out fear, because fear involves torment. But he who fears has not been made perfect in love."* That's a powerful statement! Where there is no love, there is fear and torment. But perfect love is the power that casts out the spirit of fear and torment. According to 1 John 4:17 (see the beginning of this chapter), as Jesus is, *so are we in this world.*

More times than not, our understanding and foundation of love and our relationship with our Heavenly Father have mirrored the kind of love and relationship we had/have with our earthly father. Many times I have seen people struggling to receive love from God and others because they didn't have a healthy relationship of love with their earthly father, or they had none at all, leaving them to feel orphaned. *BUT GOD!* He is a restorer of all things and is very capable of transforming our understanding of love so that His presence in our life imprints us according to *who* He is.

MY PERSONAL EXPERIENCE

I had a beautiful relationship with my earthly father. He was always loving, happy, laughing, full of wisdom, and an awesome worshiper of the Lord. I *LOVED* hanging out with him. I loved our walks to his office, the long hours of finding something to do there while he studied or counseled someone, our rides to the post office to mail a last-minute newsletter, and going into the music and Bible bookstores with him. I know that he loved my sisters, brother, and me because of how he was with us. He was always protective and watching out for our best interest, always affectionate, always holding our hands when we were walking, and wasn't afraid to hug and kiss us in public and let us know that he valued us.

Because my parents were in full-time ministry, there was no guarantee that when a plan for the family was made, we'd be able to see it to fruition, especially on weekends. So, my dad initiated "family night," which was on Monday evenings. We couldn't schedule anything on Mondays because it was reserved for spending time together. He loved to load us all in the car and take us driving, always to a surprise destination that caused us all to become more excited and loud with chatter the closer we got. I remember many times jumping out of the car and running ahead just as he would park. He always shouted with laughter, "Where are you going?"

And, I never knew because it was a surprise, *haha*. I would run back to my dad, grab his hand, and begin to walk *with* him. I always knew that we were getting close because of the grin that would come across his face. All of us would begin to scream with laughter and joy, jumping up and down just because *HE* was so happy. It might be a special ice cream shop, special restaurant, or his favorite—looking at Christmas lights during the holiday season. Because he found such joy in spending time with us, even the journey was an experience full of excitement, laughter, joy, and love. He wanted to be with us and bring joy to us because he loved us. Most of the time, these were just simple family outings, but he made sure we all had quality, intimate time together because he was love *to* us.

That's how our Heavenly Father is. He receives joy simply because we desire to be with Him through everything, even the journey. He loves when we take the initiative to grab His hand and let Him lead us in life. Because He *is love to us*, He smiles and grins with joy and excitement as He finds us receiving and experiencing true love and joy from Him.

> *Numbers 6:25 "The Lord make His face shine upon you, And be gracious to you;"*

The ERV version of the Bible says it like this: *"May the Lord smile down on you and show you his kindness."* Contrary to how I thought for many years of my life, GOD is happy and loving and wants to bless me for receiving his love, not rain down His wrath on me for bad behavior.

I never had a problem receiving love from my dad, even when I had messed up or disobeyed. Yes, I was scared to get into trouble because he had this look that only he could do, and when his voice would become very stern, that immediately let us know we were misbehaving. But all in all, even his discipline never caused me to question his love for me because the relationship between us was established in love. We didn't have a naughty spot or a time-out bench. We knew "Mr. Brown Belt" and "Mr. Black Belt." They were quite effective in getting his message of correction across to us. Out of receiving my father's love for me came trust, joy, peace, safety, stability, and respect for myself and others. I realize now that I was experiencing Abba's love through my earthly father's example of how much he had received Father God. Even in the correction, I could receive because he always moved in love. Our Heavenly Father chastens those He loves, and when we are in a time of correction, or realignment, we need to embrace the entire moment so that we continue to grow in the likeness of Christ Jesus.

> *Hebrews 12:6-7 "'For whom the Lord loves He chastens, And scourges every son whom He receives.' If you endure chastening, God deals with you as with sons; for what son is there whom a father does not chasten?"*

> *Romans 8:29 "For whom He foreknew, He also predestined to be conformed to the image of His Son…."*

Not too long ago, I had a wonderful experience that has reminded me of the Heavenly Father's love for me. I wasn't feeling well, and as I was lying down, I began to think of my life from the beginning until now ~ literally. My thoughts drifted to a time when I was thirty-five, raising three boys (9, 11, and 13 years old). After sixteen years of marriage, I had recently separated from my husband, and I was angry, hurt, and devastated. I didn't know what my future held. I still loved my Heavenly Father, but as I allowed bitterness to enter my life, I began to feel further and further from Him. I tried to throw myself in my work to be fulfilled by success, and I even tried going out with co-workers and partying when the boys were with their dad, but I never seemed to fit in with what was going on around me, and I was feeling more and more disconnected from Father God.

As I remembered those days, Holy Spirit gave me a visual of what that particular time in my life looked like in the spirit realm. I saw me, in all my bitterness and hurt, being held so tightly by my Heavenly Father that even if I had wanted to get out of His grip, I couldn't. I literally felt His arms around me, and Holy Spirit whispered in my ear. "Even then, I couldn't let you go; my love was saturating you." Immediately, I had the revelation that He

From the place of receiving God's love, we can become love to ourselves first.

had never taken His love away from me. My struggle was in my receiving His love for me during those moments when I felt so disconnected from Him and out of place, I was the one who tried to pull away not Him.

BE LOVE

The Word of God is clear that nothing can separate us from the Father's love, Romans 8:38-39 *"For I am persuaded that neither death nor life, nor angels nor principalities nor powers, nor things present nor things to come, nor height nor depth, nor any other created thing, shall be able to separate us from the love of God which is in Christ Jesus our Lord."* We have a promise that His love will always saturate every fiber of our being. The problem is *allowing* the Father's love to conquer our thoughts, our will, and our emotions. We must relent and surrender our thoughts, will, and emotions to His love. We must decide that His Spirit in us is greater than what our soul (our thoughts, will, and emotions) understands. Because we know, according to 1 John 4:18, there is no fear in love, and if I fear, love has not been perfected in me, I needed to ask myself one simple question: "Am I afraid to relent and surrender my thoughts, will, and emotions to His love?" Because if I am, then I haven't been made perfect in love, and that sent me on a journey to perfect love. My greatest desire is to be made perfect in the love of God and this is my promise!

Love is the answer to every kind of conflict that we face in our world today. In the 90s, Christian music group The Jackson Family sang a song called "Let Love BE Love," and no truer words were ever written! It is our responsibility as the people of God to let *LOVE BE LOVE* and not try to define it with our thoughts and opinions. As we receive love, we will *be* love effortlessly as God loves through us.

God is revealing His love to many people right now, and His love is not limited by a particular race, culture, or belief system. Jesus is manifesting Himself to all, even the unsaved and unchurched throughout the world and the Body of Christ, so that His revival of truth ignites in our hearts like wildfire across the globe and brings reformation to the Body of Christ through His love. We are already experiencing the greatest revival of all as we allow God to reveal Himself to us and through us individually. We can be love to others and never utter a word, and they'll come to Christ just because they experienced His glory of love.

Look at these six scriptures in Ephesians 3:14-19. "*For this reason I bow my knees to the Father of our Lord Jesus Christ, from whom the* ***whole family in heaven and earth is named****, that He would grant you, according to the riches of His glory,* ***to be strengthened with might through His Spirit in the inner man****, that Christ may dwell in your hearts through faith; that you,* ***being rooted and grounded in love****, may be able to comprehend with all the saints what is the width and length and depth and height—****to know the love of Christ which passes knowledge; that you may be filled with all the fullness of God.***"

When Christians have accepted and believed the truth that God recognizes us as those of His own family, we have completely entrusted ourselves (our thoughts, our will, and our emotions) to Abba Father. Then, He roots and grounds us in love to truly know love and to be filled with the fullness of God ~ LOVE.

Friend, you may be lying in a sickbed or have no energy to physically stand, or you may be so discouraged and depressed that you have even contemplated suicide. But, know this, when you have received the precious love of God, you will be strong enough, because you have the fullness of God, to allow the Word of God, Jesus, to come forth amid doubt and fear. He will be *STANDING AND DECLARING IN THE SPIRIT REALM, AND THE ENEMY SEES, HEARS AND FLEES!*

> *John 1:1 "In the beginning was the Word, and the Word was with God, and* ***the Word was God."***
>
> *John 1:14 "And* ***the Word became flesh and dwelt among us****, and we beheld His glory, the glory as of* ***the only begotten of the Father****, full of grace and truth."*

From the place of receiving God's love, we can become love to ourselves first. We must love ourselves enough to allow Jesus to come into our reality, so His transforming Spirit continues to work in us, making it possible to receive God's best for us right where we are in the middle of the circumstance. Simply allowing the Word of God to come forth in the midst of trouble, worry, fear, and heartache creates the atmosphere to be electrified by the all-consuming love and protection of our Heavenly Father. In that space, He brings all things into alignment to His Spirit where love is received, hope is restored, and He makes all things new.

Chapter 3

HERE COMES THE BRIDE

Identity is important for everyone. Knowing who we are is vital to our success and prospering in all things. But, more important than us knowing who we are as individuals and creating an identity for ourselves is knowing who Father God says we are and allowing Holy Spirit to define our identity in Him.

According to 3 John 2, *"Beloved, I pray that you may prosper in all things and be in health just as your soul prospers."* God calls us *beloved*. The word "beloved" in this scripture comes from the Greek word *agapētos, which* means *beloved, esteemed, dear, favorite, and* ***worthy of love***. Abba Father deems us as worthy of His love, and that fact alone tells us that He identifies us with Jesus and the price He paid for us. This is the foundation on which God builds everything in our lives ~ HIS LOVE FOR US! He doesn't begin by looking at our sin nature and assessing if He *can* love us. No, He is mindful of the salvation that He provided for all of us through the obedience of Jesus Christ. This fact is the ONE distinction that perfects His love in us. It is our responsibility for the health and wholeness of who we are and our identity to receive and accept God's truth about us...that we are worthy of love! We can't do anything to lose His love, but we can choose not to receive it.

Jesus, God's only son, came to earth to pay the ultimate price for all of our sin, sickness, *dis*-ease, *dis*-order, *dis*-appointment, *dis*-traction, *dis*-illusion, and *dis*-couragement. Consider all the *dis*-es that HE annihilated at the cross. The ultimate exchange was made for us to receive wholeness, health, wealth, and more than enough grace *(favor)* for a whole, abundant life. He took all the pain away from us now and from our future. NO MORE, IT IS FINISHED, FINAL! The only way to become who He is, which is our privilege and purpose, is to be joined to Him, become *ONE IN HIM,* and understand that we are no longer identified by our sin but by the righteousness of Jesus because we have received the precious gift of salvation from Father God.

Romans 7:4 says, *"Therefore, my brethren, you also have become dead to the law through the body of Christ, that* ***you may be married to another****—to Him who was raised [Jesus Christ] from the dead, that we should bear fruit to God."* When we give our lives to Christ, we leave law and marry grace!

Ephesians 5:25-27 directs us. *"Husbands, love your wives,* ***just as Christ also loved the church*** *and* ***gave Himself for her****, that He might sanctify and cleanse her with the washing of water by the word, that He might present her to Himself a glorious church, not having spot or wrinkle or any such thing, but that she should be holy and without blemish."*

We are no longer identified by our sin but by the righteousness of Jesus.

Listen, beloved friend. Christ did *EVERYTHING* to make it possible for us to be one with Himself and bring us into His realm of living gloriously every day! But, we must receive this gift by allowing Him to do it. We must humble ourselves to receive His *love* because it is in His loving us that we are washed clean with His Word and have a new identity! Jesus' love that qualifies us as His is only useful if we receive it. When we truly understand the exchange made for us at the cross and receive that exchange, we are giving ourselves to God's marriage covenant because we are *FULLY* giving ourselves to Christ. We choose to give up our old nature and receive the righteous nature of Jesus, and Father God now recognizes us as being one with Jesus. To truly be committed to being ONE FLESH with Jesus, we must posture ourselves daily to receive HIM.......we must surrender and submit our will to become empty of self so that all we have to offer and pour out to anyone is Jesus Christ Himself. It is our responsibility to LET HIM COME FORTH! Galatians 2:20 says, *"I have been crucified with Christ; it is no longer I who live,* **but Christ lives in me**; *and the life which I now live in the flesh I live by faith in the Son of God, who loved me and gave Himself for me."*

There once was a time when a bride depended on her husband for everything. She understood that she needed his care, and for her to receive his care, she had to surrender all that she had ever known from living with her parents and receive from her husband with a submissive heart, yielding to him in trust. In return, the husband knew that his wife's love for him was steadfast and given freely without demand. They made plans together to bring forth children (the fruit of their union), and their life together was built on a foundation of hopes, dreams, and the giving of themselves to one another in faith and trust for *love's* sake. There was an understanding that they had joined themselves together to build a new life that would identify them as one entity and no longer two. My heart rejoices when I speak with couples who have been married 40, 50, and 60 years. They all have one thing in common: they *meant* what they said at the altar and took their vows seriously on their wedding day. They didn't have Plan B; Plan A HAD TO WORK! Sadly, that's not the overall picture of marriage in today's world. I have witnessed a mindset about marriage that projects equality between the man and woman, identifying as equally the same, 50/50 instead of identifying as *ONE FLESH,* and being a 100% whole union.

Some will argue whether or not the Body of Christ is indeed the Bride of Christ. Still, I must say that I believe I am the Bride of Christ because *I have given myself* to Jesus Christ according to Romans 7:4," *Therefore, my brethren, you also have become dead to the law through the body of Christ, that you may be married to another—to Him who was raised from the dead, that we should bear fruit to God."*.

Accepting grace means that I have entered covenant marriage...*ONE FLESH* with Jesus Christ, who *is* grace. This surrender to Christ must begin in us individually, and then we all find ourselves in unity as the Holy Spirit brings us together through His perfected love. The enemy is always looking for an opportunity to draw us away from this truth and separate, isolate and divide us hoping to get us focused on our will, our way, and our effort.

A constant strategy of the enemy is to get us focused on a problem and then fill our mind and head with thoughts of how *we* can resolve it out of our effort. God doesn't focus on the problem; in fact, He doesn't ever see "problems." He has given His Word to us, and He knows His Word is LIFE to all the issues that we face in our earthly journey. Remember that a posture of complete surrender and yielding to Him is the only answer, receiving and submitting to His will, way, and effort. Drawing into His Word and allowing Him to speak and move on our behalf when we face challenges is the beginning of our identity changing from an individual to becoming one flesh in Christ. We must allow our bridegroom to love, cherish, and take care of us as He perfects His love in us. The Word of God is the way to *know* our bridegroom and understand who He is in us.

The Bride of Christ is made up of all of us who have believed John 1:14, which says, "*And the Word became flesh and dwelt among us, and we beheld His glory, the glory as of the only begotten of the Father, full of **grace** and truth.*"

The Bride of Christ is beginning to emerge graceful and loving towards all with a voice that trumpets the unfailing love of our groom. We are beginning to recognize the importance of His mercy and compassion in our journey as we meet others on the road of life. We are called to be the good in someone's bad day, and by the love and power of God, we are witnessing miracles of healing, deliverance, and breakthrough for many. The Bride of Christ is gaining her momentum as she strives less to become what the world desires, but rather to understand who she is because of the love given to her through Christ Jesus. She pleases her bridegroom as she allows His love and grace to be seen and felt by others. She is becoming *like* Him. The Bride of Christ has come to the end of herself and her ability and has accepted and received her identity through the Word of God. The Bride of Christ is becoming more and more fortified and strong as she is cleansed by the washing of the Word of God continuously, *"Husbands, love your wives, just as* ***Christ also loved the church and gave Himself for her, that He might sanctify and cleanse her with the washing of water by the word,*** *that He might present her to Himself a glorious church, not having spot or wrinkle or any such thing, but that she should be holy and without blemish."* ~ Ephesians 5:25 & 26.

You are everything
the Word of God
says you are.

The Bride of Christ is bearing the fruits of love, joy, peace, patience, kindness, goodness, gentleness, faithfulness, and self-control. Yes, our fruit is the product of our union with Christ. When we begin to exhibit these fruits, we know that Christ is becoming greater in us than our limited natural self. There is a SUPERnatural exchange taking place. His thoughts are replacing our thoughts, His will has replaced our will, and His emotions are becoming our emotions.

Beloved friend, I want to challenge you to allow this truth to sink in as you are reading. You are *EVERYTHING* the Word of God says you are. You are blessed and highly favored of God! And, simply because you have surrendered your life to Christ and recognize that you (male and female) are the beloved one, the Bride of Christ, you live a life of wholeness because God CHOSE YOU, and you said “YES” to Him.

Chapter 4

LEAVE AND CLEAVE

In the previous chapter, I explained who the *Bride of Christ* is and how she is moving in the earth, gaining momentum as she loves selflessly and genuinely cares for others with compassion and mercy. For the Bride to be true in Christ's likeness, she must understand and know the true principle of leaving and cleaving ~ leaving the old (self) to cleave to the new (Christ). The leaving is, for the most part, simply "going away from," but the cleaving can prove to be an impossibility on our part because that word means to *split or sever, to make a way through something forcibly*, but with God, it is a possibility.

Many of us have generational ideas, traditional ways that have worked for us all our lives, strong beliefs that we have held on to (sometimes to our own demise), and thought processes that must be forcibly split and severed to receive the love of God and become one who reflects that love on the earth. We can gain understanding and strength to cleave when we truly recognize who Jesus is and what He did when He was made flesh requiring Him to leave Heaven, come to earth, and dwell among us.

The fact that God was made flesh and dwelt among us is almost hard to conceive in this day and age if we allow our minds to be shaped by the world around us. I often tell people if they want to begin their journey of understanding who Jesus is, then they need to read the four gospels ~ Matthew, Mark, Luke, and John. In these four books of the Bible, a clear picture is painted for us to see who Jesus truly is, how he handled tough situations, endured hate and rejection, gave *FULLY* of Himself despite doubters, and moved according to the leading of Holy Spirit throughout the earth. Jesus showed us what it looks like to live in alignment with Father God, and He is not an exception, but rather the greatest example we have of what is possible for us from Jesus' perspective. Look at John 5:19 with me: *"Then Jesus answered and said to them, "Most assuredly, I say to you,* ***the Son can do nothing of Himself, but what He sees the Father do..."*** Did you catch that? Jesus only did what He had witnessed the Father do. He did not devise His own plan or even come in His own strength. He did not move about the earth pouring out to people good things and blessings because He thought it would be a good idea. NO! He came in the leading and power of the Holy Ghost and the love of His Father. He came as Heavenly Father with legs. So all that He did was because He was full of Father God and complete in Him.

Every part of who Jesus is, what Jesus did, and what Jesus spoke is our standard as Believers in this crazy world we live in. Through faith and humility, this standard becomes our reality, making us whole.

WHAT FATHER GOD DESIRES

We understand who our Heavenly Father is and get a glimpse of His heart desire through watching the life Jesus lived when he was here. We also see His heart's desire in the book of Exodus, when the ten commandments were first given to Moses by God the Father for the people. They were given in hopes that the people of God would see how much they needed Him. Without Him, they would be sick, lame, lacking, withered, and paralyzed in their minds even after being delivered from Egypt. They were physically delivered out of Egypt, but their minds were still in bondage to an old way. Simply put, because they were slaves while in Egypt, they had a slave mentality to depend on man. God's desire was for His people to look to Him and trust Him in His goodness, knowing that He loved them and wanted their dependence to be on Him.

Through scripture, we can witness the intense longing God has to be known by His people, and He gave the law to show them how much they needed Him. God knew they couldn't keep the law in their own ability. God knew that they were to be identified as *HIS OWN* people...not the people of Egypt! His greatest desire was to show them how much He loved them and wanted to be their God and lead them so they could *rest in Him,* Matthew 11:28 *"Come to Me, all you who labor and are heavy laden, and I will give you rest."* God's desire STILL is for us to know who we are in Him and allow Him to bring us into an intimate relationship with Him where all His promises are fulfilled and manifested in our life and we live in true rest.

He has always known that being fully delivered out of a place of bondage demands a mind shift (a severing of wrong thinking and wrong beliefs) to come into a new place of freedom in God. He knew all along what He was doing and how Jesus would come to redeem the Children of Israel from what they couldn't see, understand, or uphold on their own. Throughout the Old Testament, we see glimpses of the same message: the Son of God would come and do for us what we cannot do for ourselves. In the labor of keeping the ten commandments, there was always the fear of a curse or death if they broke one.

When Jesus comes to the earth, He comes as the love, mercy, and grace of our Heavenly Father, not to point out where everyone has broken the law and failed in their ability. Jesus delivers a message of Father's unconditional love through every word of love and hope and every act of salvation and healing he did on the earth.

WALK AWAY

There's a story in John 5 that tells of Jesus healing a man on the Sabbath who had an infirmity for thirty-eight years. Once a year, the angel of the Lord would come and stir the waters in the pool at Bethesda, and whoever stepped into the water first was healed of their infirmity. When Jesus asked this man if he wanted to be made well, the man answered that for 38 years, when the waters were stirred, there was no one to put him in the water so he could be healed. He had to depend on others to help him into the water first so he would be healed. Jesus spoke right over the man's answer, saying, "Rise, take up your bed and walk!" He healed the man of his infirmity, the man became well, he could walk again, he was set free of pain, and he was set free of depending on others (a form of bondage).

The religious leaders considered Jesus to be working on the Sabbath, the day of rest. They couldn't see the wellness and freedom which the man had received because they were focused on the *do's* and *don'ts* of the law, and they questioned Jesus' integrity because, in their understanding, He had broken the fourth commandment of the law of resting on Sabbath. In reality, Jesus had just brought the man *into* Himself, who is perfect rest and wholeness and freedom. Jesus' actions sent the message that HE IS THE LORD OF SABBATH, meaning *HE IS REST*. If Jesus only did what He saw His Father do, then the Father broke the natural law of Sabbath-keeping. Jesus fulfilled the supernatural law of Sabbath REST! The deeper truth of Sabbath is Father God wants to bring His people into His rest because He desires a relationship. He's not up in Heaven watching to see who is obeying the natural law now because Jesus has come and fulfilled ALL the law. He desires our hearts turned towards Him in a relationship with Him. Matthew 12:8, *"For the Son of Man is Lord even of the Sabbath."* With Jesus being Lord of Sabbath, He has provided the way for us to remain and live in the place of rest and peace. When he healed the man, His actions demonstrate the love of Abba Father and deliver the message that God's love supersedes the natural by fulfilling the supernatural nature of Heavenly Father. In the Spirit, Jesus already saw the man whole, healthy, and prospering while resting in the unfailing love of Jesus Christ.

Sabbath is the day of rest, and there's no greater example of resting than *receiving* the gift of grace and freedom through Jesus' love. In Heaven, Jesus witnessed His father, full of love, mercy, and grace, make a way of escape for the children of Israel; a sick, lame, withered, lacking, and paralyzed nation. He awakened them to a new mindset of who they really were and to the possibility of a true place of promise and freedom that is

*Jesus moved in love
and compassion,
not religious order.*

real. The law pointed the people to God and put a demand on **them** to uphold it, but now because of Jesus, His love saturates us and is given freely 100% to all who simply receive it, allowing Jesus to fulfill the law in our life with no demand or effort on our part. We only must allow Him to *be* Jesus and receive Him.

The man who Jesus healed had to *receive* what Jesus was offering:

- Concerning the man, his circumstances were beyond his control, and they had become his focus: what he *wasn't able* to do and what he *didn't have*.
- His infirmity had become his bed or place of resting.
- The man was in bondage to others because of his dependency on them to help him be first in the water.

Jesus saw beyond the natural condition when He asked him if he wanted to be made well. He knew how long he had been that way before he even spoke and asked the man, "Do you want to be made well? John 5:6 *"When Jesus saw him lying there, and knew that he already had been in that condition a long time, He said to him, "Do you want to be made well?".*

The man began to answer from his natural perspective and understanding of his circumstances; his words stated **why** he was not well. Jesus responded from **knowing the possibility in Himself** and didn't even address what seems impossible to the man. Jesus has offered a renewed life, strength, rest, and abundance through Himself and gave the instruction, "Rise, take up your bed and walk."

Jesus moved in love and compassion, not religious order. Jesus is the way to move forward into the undiscovered life of freedom from bondage and away from the religion/law that limits us and keeps us within the boundaries of our thinking, believing, and effort. The Bible says that *immediately* the man was made well. He didn't question Jesus' instructions but obeyed, and he received his immediate healing and deliverance from the bondage of his bed and his circumstance. He no longer depended on others to help him be first (oh reader, I HOPE YOU JUST GRABBED THAT NUGGET!!), and his 38-year-old problem of infirmity no longer identified him as a paralytic. At the very moment that Jesus healed him, there was an exchange happening. The man chose to **leave** and walk away from what he had known for 38 years, everything that defined him, and he **cleaved** to Jesus who gave him a new identity, set him free from bondage, and gifted him a life of redemption and fullness in Him.

Friend, we have every reason to pause, thank and praise God right now for His love, mercy, and grace, which is given freely to us because He has made a way of escape (changed our identity) from bondage to freedom through Jesus Christ. The scriptures have been given to us as a testament of God's desire to have a restored relationship with us. If you've been doubting yourself or have questions of this fulfilled life in Christ, open the Word of God and begin to saturate your spirit with His *WORD* which is *LIFE*. I hope you will gain clarity and understanding through the truth of the transformational journey of identity that begins when we say NO to self and YES to God.

Sometimes it is a simple matter of leaving the familiar comfort of our thinking and cleaving by faith to what we've never known through Jesus' Words. Jesus said to the man, "Pick up that bed that you've been lying in for thirty-eight years, begin to walk and go forward! Forget all that didn't go right in your life, cleave to me, walk in My way, and see what I will do."

How many times have we heard, "They made their bed, so they have to lie in it." What a LIE from the enemy!!! Jesus says, "NO WAY! Get up out of that misery, even if you have created it, and draw into me, believe My Word and obey it, cleave to ME your PROMISE as you leave the PROBLEM. What looks impossible to you is **possible** with Me!"

WALK THIS WAY

One of the greatest struggles that I've witnessed among the Body of Christ is to remain faith-filled and live according to faith. Our culture and society in the United States have created, established, and prioritized self-dependent, self-reliant, and sterile systems to live (the job and paycheck, status in society, health insurance, car insurance, 401K retirement fund, the IRS, etc.). The GREATEST joy in life is KNOWING that God has us in the palm of His hand, and faith is alive inside of us. If all the systems made by man (the job and paycheck, status in society, health insurance, car insurance, 401K retirement fund, the IRS, etc) have become our focus to maintain security and stability, we have missed it. I'm not saying that these things aren't important because they are, and some of them are the law of the land. But, I am saying that if they have erased the need to live by faith and trust God in our lives, then our spirit is not in alignment with Him. Hebrews 12:2 says, *"...looking unto Jesus, the author and finisher of our faith..."*. We are to focus on Jesus; everything begins and ends in Him. Jesus *is* faith, and the Bible says that the righteous/justified live by faith.

Romans 1:17 says, *"For in it the righteousness of God is revealed from faith to faith; as it is written, "The just shall live by faith."*

Galatians 3:11 emphasizes, *"But that no one is justified by the law in the sight of God is evident, for "the just shall live by faith."*

Hebrews 10:38 states, *"Now the just shall live by faith; but if anyone draws back, My soul has no pleasure in him."*

We walk by faith, not by sight, and faith is the avenue to righteousness. Let me say it this way: the righteous/justified live according to Jesus. We walk according to Jesus' way. We walk according to Jesus' sight, not according to what we see naturally. I think it's safe to say that according to scripture, we must live and be driven by faith, not by the systems of the world designed for our success. We must be Jesus-conscious more than we are conscious of what we can make work. We must leave a mindset that is limited by our ability and effort and cleave to a consciousness of Jesus that is limitless because of who He is and know that He is working through us. **All of *our* systems**

must come into alignment according to our faith ~ not our faith coming into alignment according to our systems.

Another major area of thinking that the Body of Christ must leave is the *law* mindset; we must cleave to the *grace mindset*. A law mentality will put demands on *our* effort and our ability *to do* something that we believe makes us worthy and entitled before God. But a grace mentality takes away all self-effort and ability on our part; it says to God that we understand we are nothing without Him. Ephesians 2:8 & 9 *"For by grace you have been saved through faith, and that not of yourselves; it is the gift of God, not of works, lest anyone should boast."* We must simply humble ourselves and *receive* from Him.

Most of the man-made church systems that have been in place for hundreds of years throughout many denominations have screamed that for us to come to God, we must clean ourselves up according to a set of instructions and demands. Only then will He receive us. WRONG!!! How can this be if the Word of God itself says that even our righteousness is like filthy rags to our Heavenly Father?

> *Isaiah 64:6 "But we are all like an unclean thing, And all our righteousnesses are like filthy rags; We all fade as a leaf, And our iniquities, like the wind, Have taken us away."*

The truth is that God did not say we had to clean up before coming to Him, but some spiritual leadership has said that. They have implied not only to clean up before presenting ourselves to God but also to stay clean to have the right to continue to come to Him. Here are just a few examples of what has been taught:

- Dress a certain way
- Make sure we go to church

- Pay tithes and offerings (this is wrong because the correct word is to *return* our tithe)
- Don't smoke
- Don't drink
- Don't cuss or chew
- Don't be caught associating with those who do any of the above.

Over the years, the man-made system of church has caused us to focus on the outward nature when God has always looked at our heart and focused on our spiritual nature because He is concerned that *we become The Church*. He has always known this to be our true identity.

According to His Word He knows our heart and intent, and He focuses on those two things, giving us everything we need through Jesus to bring us to a redemptive place in Him by grace. In the book of Corinthians, Paul shares with us that he dealt with "a thorn in his flesh" that he could not get rid of. The Word of God does not tell us what that thorn was, but it DOES tell us that the precious gift of grace is sufficient for anything we deal with. 2 Corinthians 12:8 & 9 *"Concerning this thing I pleaded with the Lord three times that it might depart from me. And He said to me, "My* ***grace is sufficient*** *for you, for My strength is made perfect in weakness." Therefore most gladly I will rather boast in my infirmities, that the power of Christ may rest upon me."* Paul says that the power of God rests upon him even in his infirmity! THAT IS POWERFUL AND COMFORTING! Even when we do not know ourselves the intent of our heart, God does and He has made sure we have the grace needed to power through the weakness because of the strength of Jesus Christ. Grace is an internal dynamic between our spirit and Jesus Christ and is so simple because we must only receive it. This truth has threatened the church as a whole, so it tries to steer clear of it.

Over the last fifteen years or so, there has been a great grace revolution emerging in the Body of Christ, the true Church. For the most part, the religious system has tried to silence the voice of those who carry the message. The system has made grace conditional. Some denominations have even prohibited leadership from preaching about it, reading books about it, and even having conversations about it. Grace takes all control away from man who is looking on the outward and places each individual in a capsule with God Himself, allowing the redemption of all the life issues to be between *"me and God"* only. Many leaders have even taught that the message of grace is giving God's people a *license to sin*, but the truth is that it is completely the opposite.

Grace gives God's people the *power* to overcome the challenging issues they face and not give into sin. When we truly understand His grace and how we are transformed when we receive it, we don't want to sin. If we simply receive from Jesus what we cannot do for ourselves ~ grace to live free from sin, we immediately experience peace that passes all of our understanding. Beyond what makes sense to us when we receive God's grace, we receive supernatural energy to believe that something better is awaiting us even if the circumstances haven't changed yet. The posture of receiving grace is humility; understanding that we can do nothing in our effort. We must rely totally on the power and strength of Holy Spirit to bring us through these challenging issues.

Our pride says, "I will conquer this even if it kills me!" Moving in pride like this too many times will bring a person to a place of spiritual death, and they will stay there until the Spirit of Jesus resurrects them. It takes a humble person to be in the midst of the *sin nature* and profess that they are the righteousness of God through Christ Jesus. When our posture is humility, and we have *received* God's grace, pride is gone.

Each of us is in a process called *life* to bring us to that place where we continually receive God's grace. We are on a journey to destiny ~ *yes*, but the greatest discoveries and breakthroughs in life are found in the journey, not the destination. When we leave our old self (old thinking, old ways) and cleave to a new self (new thinking and new ways) through Jesus, we receive what God has wanted to give us all along - His love and grace.

It takes a humble person to be in the midst of the sin nature and profess that they are the righteousness of God through Christ Jesus.

THE MODEL

I know the concept of "each man for himself with God" could imply that God's people don't need leadership and are left vulnerable, but this couldn't be further from the truth. We, as a body, need leadership, but we need true Kingdom leadership designed by God. The structure is of the five-fold ministry, not in title only but functionality as we allow the love of God through His Spirit to minister to His people. The gifts of apostle, prophet, evangelist, pastor, and teacher is the Kingdom structure modeled through the life of Jesus throughout the New Testament. The five-fold ministry in title only is nothing and ineffective.

At some point, we embraced the idea of giving the "leader" position to one person called the pastor/shepherd set behind a pulpit. We have expected that person to watch over the sheep, keep them clean and spot-free, and keep them corralled so they won't wander into another pasture. Many pastors even believe that God put them in a position to be the Holy Spirit and police His people.

Wow! How wrong we have been in our thinking and our expectation of the man (or woman) on earth behind a pulpit. We have thought that we were doing all the good works and monitoring others through a religious system for Father God in Heaven! There has been a severe breakdown in our understanding of God's Kingdom blueprint given to us in the life of Jesus.

God has a plan, and He is at work executing it through His people, HIS CHURCH, now throughout the earth. As His plan is being carried out and bringing alignment and order according to His Word, the death sentence of old, wrong systems of thinking, believing, expectations, and leadership of his people is being executed. Believers are leaving and cleaving to God's Kingdom dynamic. Jesus is taking back His Church as His people receive His love and grace on a personal level. We are leaving an old way that brought us the consciousness of knowing our sin-nature and cleaving to the consciousness of knowing our Spirit-nature, our righteousness in Jesus.

God has provided a way out of the sin nature for all of us but it is determined by our will to receive His gifts of love, grace, and mercy. The question which we must all ask is, "Will I leave the limitations I've always known to cleave to someone who is limitless in His love for me and desires to give me a life of abundance in spirit, soul, and body?" My answer is yes, and if your answer is yes, then we are living in the supernatural flow of God's Spirit, joining Him on His journey of life with the assurance that He is fulfilling purpose in us because we chose to leave and cleave.

Chapter 5

VERTICAL BEFORE HORIZONTAL

Before God can move through us to others, we must allow Him to move *IN* us, and for that to happen, we must allow ourselves to become more than just an occasional acquaintance with Father God. We must shore up our vertical relationship with our Heavenly Father before our horizontal relationships with others will be of any value.

Picture in your mind what it looked like when Jesus hung on a cross being crucified. His arms stretched out to each side as The Roman soldiers nailed Him at his feet and His hands. On His right and His left hung two criminals, each being crucified as well. In Luke 23, we read that one of the criminals blasphemes Jesus, and the other criminal rebukes him. That criminal says to Jesus, *"Lord, remember me when you come into your Kingdom."* ~ Luke 23:42. And Jesus replies, *"Assuredly I say to you, today you will be with me in Paradise."* ~ Luke 23:43. How is it that all three of these men are experiencing the same agony of crucifixion, and Jesus can release a promise like that to one of the two criminals who were horizontal to Him?

The answer is simple. Before He ever reached Golgotha for crucifixion, He was prepared in His Spirit because He had spent the time needed with His Heavenly Father, He was prepared vertically. Throughout the New Testament, we read many accounts of Jesus withdrawing from the crowds to pray to the Father on His own. All four gospels tell us that before Jesus was arrested, He had gone to the garden to pray and release His will to Father God. Matthew 26:39 *"He went a little farther and fell on His face, and prayed, saying, "O My Father, if it is possible, let this cup pass from Me; nevertheless, not as I will, but as You will."* Jesus demonstrates that to be effective horizontally (as when He spoke a promise to the one criminal), we must first be spiritually connected vertically to our Heavenly Father. Remember, Jesus is God in flesh form, and in His love, He came to earth to give us His divinity in exchange for our humanity. Love itself brings the power to lay down our own will, and like Jesus, we must be intentional about our need to spend time with Father God. Until we are able to release our own will, it is impossible for us to effectively love others with the same love that Jesus loves us.

A vertical relationship was the first relationship established between God and Adam. When Adam and Eve's disobedience violated that relationship, it separated them, and the rest of us from that relationship with God. When Adam and Eve decided to listen to the devil (they allowed the devil's voice to be louder than the voice of Father God), they forgot their righteous authority, and the enemy took advantage of it! Because they ate the fruit of the tree of the knowledge of good and evil, their eyes were opened to the natural. They began to see everything, good and bad, all things that are in opposition to the tree of life which is ALL BLESSING that God gave them to eat their fill. All of God's promises and everything good for us is in the tree of LIFE, but Adam and Eve took their focus off of life in God and focused on the tree of "knowing": the tree of the *knowledge* of good but also of poverty, disease, sickness, hatred, bitterness, pain, and loss in the earth. They began to focus horizontally and no longer vertically.

I've wondered why God didn't just throw the devil out of the garden and restore to Adam and Eve what He had given them. God is a just God, a right God, and He is love and His desire was and still is to restore through His love all of us back to Himself. From the beginning, God's intention for Adam and Eve was to only eat from and experience the fruit of the tree of life. But because of the serpent's cunning deception, they ate the fruit of the tree of knowledge of good and evil. God never wanted them to know the heartache of evil, but they insisted. It had to

Until we are able to release our own will, it is impossible for us to effectively love others with the same love that Jesus loves us.

be their decision to choose God and trust His love and His best for them even when He gave the instruction NOT to eat the fruit of the tree of knowledge.

When Jesus shed his blood and was crucified and resurrected, He provided full restoration of garden living to those who willfully receive Him in His totality and live according to His Spirit. We are restored to the tree of life when we choose to focus vertically. Our vertical relationship is restored through Jesus, and now we thrive from that place of communion with our Heavenly Father.

Our relationship with Him and its nurturing must become our daily priority, daily focus, and daily motivation to live. I can honestly say that for as long as I can remember, Father God has been the first one I speak to when I open my eyes in the morning and the last one I speak to when going to sleep. Because my vertical relationship with Father God is my top priority, I have all confidence that God is ever-present in my life and that He is tangibly close at all times.

PROCESS TO PROCEED

Psalm 37:23 says, *"The steps of a good man are ordered by the Lord, and He delights in his ways."* If we know that we are the righteousness of God through Jesus (a good man), then we have the assurance that God is ordering our steps. Life is about our steps that make the journey ~ the whole journey ~ that begins at conception. Like a daisy chain, all of our experiences and moments link together to bring us to our destiny in God for *HIS* purpose.

Some people refer to the journey as a process, and that is a true statement. A process has a beginning with an expected outcome, and in-between the beginning and outcome, we go through trials, challenges, difficulties, twists, and turns that develop and grow us and quite often bring change. When we don't allow our vertical relationship with Father God to process us, we stunt our growth in becoming who He sees we are and who He has called us to be. It is a sad truth that many people spend most of their lives trying to "set" everything in their lives so that they don't have to go through the process, giving birth to all the man-made systems, formulas, and methods in our culture.

There are horizontal systems and formulas designed for financial security, health and wellness, prosperity, and success. Our culture says to focus on someone we aspire to be like and do what they did by implementing their methods and formulas, and we will achieve the same results. Some are even consumed by an idea of who they *want to be* more than knowing who they truly are in God for His purpose. That's an invitation for a *copy-cat spirit* and can be very dangerous to our God-given destiny.

Our life trajectory must not be altered by a false sense or understanding of security and success that has been birthed by focusing horizontally on people because we have failed to nurture a life-giving relationship with Father God. Our destiny is birthed out of our vertical relationship with Him, and it must be our number one priority if we are going to be effective horizontally. We are created to be one-of-a-kind, unique, wonderful individuals who are the dwelling place of the Spirit of God, bearing His fruit and all of us carrying gifts that He wants to bring forth in us for the equipping of the whole Body, the Bride of Christ.

Our vertical life in
God is imperative
before we'll be effective
horizontally.

Psalm 139:14 "I will praise You, for I am fearfully and wonderfully made; Marvelous are Your works, And that my soul knows very well."

1Corinthians 3:16 "Do you not know that you are the temple of God and that the Spirit of God dwells in you?"

Galatians 5:22 "But the fruit of the Spirit is love, joy, peace, longsuffering, kindness, goodness, faithfulness, gentleness, self-control."

Ephesians 4:11 & 12 "And He Himself gave some to be apostles, some prophets, some evangelists, and some pastors and teachers, for the equipping of the saints for the work of ministry, for the edifying of the body of Christ."

Making time for just "God and me" is imperative if we are going to see and do what Jesus did when He walked the earth. How much we nurture our vertical relationship determines how deeply connected we are to Father God through His love. Our true identity, success, and effectiveness to others will only be obtained as we allow the crucifixion of our own thoughts, will, and emotions, and the resurrection of Jesus' Spirit in us.

If you've ever flown in an airplane, chances are you remember the safety instructions that are given by the flight attendant before take-off. When they instruct us about the oxygen mask, their instruction is that if you are with a child or a person who cannot do for themselves, put the oxygen mask on yourself first. Then, assist them with theirs. Why is that? Because you need to be able to breathe to render aid to the one you are assisting.

Well, the same principle is true in our life as Believers. We must have an ample supply of life-giving breath from God before we can even begin to think that we could help someone else. Our vertical life in God is imperative before we'll be effective horizontally.

COMMUNICATE

I hope that I didn't overwhelm you with the last few paragraphs. Everything which I shared is true AND possible! What I have just described is a life of perpetual communication with our Heavenly Father. Prayer *IS* that communication, and in the life of a Believer should be continual. Jesus stayed in constant communication with His Heavenly Father. In many portions of scripture, we read that He was found withdrawing from people to pray to Father God. Why is that? Because Jesus said in John 5:19 & 20, *"Most assuredly, I say to you, the Son can do nothing of Himself, but what He sees the Father do; for whatever He does, the Son also does in like manner."*

Jesus is our example of how to live as a Kingdom steward in the earth realm, and His life shows us how to know God's response in our everyday life. He leads by example throughout the Word of God. We have to be willing to recognize and receive the revelation that just like Jesus, God's Spirit lives in us too, and we have the same need to communicate with the Father to know His desire, design, and response in all things.

Sadly, most believers in the earth right now go to prayer as a last resort instead of their first choice. If a woman or man goes to his or her spouse as the last resort in making a decision that affects their union, we'd call them self-centered and controlling, wouldn't we? We would agree that if they are joined together in marriage through love, both should seek the other one and communicate together when making decisions.

Well, it's no different in our life with Christ. We *NEED HIM* in all things, so we *MUST* communicate with Father God and allow His Spirit to *ALWAYS* lead us! One right decision in my own thinking is still not as good as being led by the Spirit of God when I have gone to Him first and stayed in communication with Him....to hear what His words are to me that will lead me in His way. Jesus always inquired of Father God, and I should do no less (see above John 5:19 & 20).

A well-developed life of communication with Father God brings forth a fruitful life and will multiply His love and ways on the earth to others. Through me, his effectiveness is an indicator that I have given myself to converse with Him every day and walk with Him in this journey called life. As I allow Him to speak to me and listen and obey, I have the assurance that He is leading and I am simply following Him. Trust in Him is being developed as my faith is rooted in Him and nurtured because I have spent time with Him. Jesus is the seed of God planted in the earth for all mankind to be saved through His resurrection as we allow Him to root us in Him. He is the vine, and we are the branches as John 15:5 says: *"I am the vine, you are the branches. He who abides in Me, and I in him, bears much fruit; for without Me you can do nothing."*

Our greatest effectiveness in horizontal relationships will happen when our vertical relationship bears the fruit of God's love and grace that has been received and developed through communication with our loving Father. When our vertical relationship bears fruit, only then do we have something to feed others.

Chapter 6

INTIMACY IS NOT FANTASY

As believers, we must clearly understand the difference between intimacy and fantasy to position and posture our lives correctly. Intimacy with Father God is His love being poured out on us, and we receive it willingly. Song of Solomon 8:7 says, *"Many waters cannot quench love, Nor can the floods drown it....."*. In other words, God's love for us is so substantial that nothing can stop it from coming forth, and no circumstance or situation can kill it.

I know that God has us in a time of wooing and drawing us to become Jesus conscious only. We must come to the place in our thinking that wherever we are and whatever we do or say, we can envision Christ being right there in the room with us because of how tangible He is in our spirit. I must be conscious of His presence being there with me in every moment of every day. If I move through life conscious that He is there too, I will consider and choose the words I say more carefully, and I'll respond in love instead of reacting in frustration and irritation when faced with a life challenge. If I am only conscious of myself and my own effort, I will react, and that dishonors Heavenly Father because oftentimes, in the moment, my reactions are from my feelings. Still, if I pause and become conscious of Jesus' presence, I will respond in God's love effectively and bring honor to Him. Intimacy with Father God is being conscious that He is here and allowing Him to love through me.

The definition of intimacy found in Webster's Dictionary is *familiarity and closeness*. I have found that we can have intimacy in friendship; we share our most fragile experiences and thoughts with someone close to our hearts knowing that they are listening and holding tightly all that we have shared. When we hear the word intimacy, most of us immediately think of the sexual relationship between a man and a woman being alone to express their love to each other and receive love from one another in marriage. They are heart to heart communicating through loving each other. There is transparency, vulnerability, and nakedness. They are together as one, and the expression of their love is being shared in emotions, words, touch, and feelings. During these times of intimacy, a child can be conceived, a product or fruit of the two becoming one. Although this is true, as I write about intimacy in this book, I am referring to the intimacy that brings us together as one with our Heavenly Father. As I speak of intimacy with Father, I am speaking of an encounter that is even more **powerful** than the intimacy in a marriage.

Intimacy is literally being consumed with who He is as we receive His love, and our love is expressed to Him in thanksgiving, worship, and thinking only of Him. May I encourage you by telling you that when I position myself to receive from the Father, I become overwhelmed with how much He loves and accepts me just as I am? And that is disarming! I find myself being honest, truthful, and transparent with the one who already knows everything about me and who has breathed life into me. I release all my defenses to Him. I let my protective walls come down. I strip off all the layers of my outward persona and stand in His presence totally naked, undone, and unashamed. As I am postured in humility, I can now *hear* Him as He speaks to me, usually in a beautiful whisper. Tangibly being in His presence brings me to the place of truly believing Him as I hear Him say, "*For I know the thoughts that I think toward you, thoughts of peace and not of evil, to give you a future and a hope.* "~Jeremiah 29:11. I BELIEVE Him because I know that I have come honestly and boldly to Him. I haven't withheld anything from Him, and He won't withhold anything from me.

Listen, friend, spiritual intimacy with God doesn't practice birth control! No, God controls what will be birthed from our worship and alone time with Him as we surrender and yield to Him as He expresses His love for us through emotions, His Word, and His tangible presence. Intimate time spent with our Heavenly Father will produce Jesus' character that will bear His fruit and manifest signs, wonders, and miracles.

You may not be aware of it, but to go deep in God and His love is simply being honest with ourselves, acknowledging the fact that we need Him to be our father and receive His love.

We only know God when we spend time with Him, communicate with Him, and receive from Him. Our times of intimacy with Father God are the most important for our health and welfare, and our entire existence depends on it. God is moving by His love through every believer to "woo us back" to communion with Him. He desires intimacy with us because He knows that intimacy with Him brings spiritual transformation to our lives, aligning everything according to Himself.

FAKE IS DANGEROUS

The definition of fantasy is *imagination and make-believe.* Fantasy begins with imagination and can be fulfilled in many ways (thoughts, books, pictures, movies, social media, etc.) as the mind responds to feelings. Fulfilled fantasy is always self-gratification, whether it be sexual, greed, or self-serving. No Godly fruit is conceived through fantasy. Intimacy happens in the spirit, and fantasy happens in the mind or soul realm. Intimacy is fruitful, and fantasy is fruitless.

Fantasy is not real, and by definition alone, it causes us to be *fake* in Father's presence because we simply do not know

Intimacy with Father God is being conscious that He is here and allowing Him to love through me.

who He is if we've only been *acquainted* with Him. Not intimately knowing Father God leaves us wide open and vulnerable to create in our own mind what we *think* a relationship with Him is like and our expression of it. Houses of worship are full of Believers who have not taken the time to be intimate with Father God through their worship and alone time with him, and they have become dependent on a corporate experience with the "right" song and dance to know that they have been in God's presence. We see fantasy being played out every week on a platform full of bells and whistles that touch people's senses and emotions. Many have accepted the feeling of emotions to be the presence of God. There is a huge difference between having an emotional experience by hearing the sound of worship and an intimate encounter when we have heard Father's voice whisper in our ear. Here's the truth: When we receive the revelation that **we carry** His presence because we are intimate with Him and we cultivate and nurture our relationship with Him, we understand "wherever I am His presence is there because I have brought Him with me." Fantasy must be worked up, but intimacy is constant and causes us to carry a Heavenly aroma that permeates the atmosphere. When leadership has that moment of discovery of true intimacy with Father God because they have been consumed by His love and received it in times of transparency with Father God, the Love of God will begin to explode in our pulpits and allow His people to be freed from the bonds of religious fantasy. Otherwise, if they never discover true intimacy with Father God, they run the risk of staying caught in the bondage of fake religious experiences.

JOY AND PROTECTION

Two major deficiencies I witness in The Church is real joy and peace in the life of many Believers. If we cultivate an intimate relationship with Father God, we have a promise that we will live in joy. *"In His presence is FULLNESS of JOY..."* ~ Psalm 16:11. And Philippians 4:7 says, "A*nd the peace of God, which surpasses all understanding, will guard your hearts and minds through Christ Jesus."* There is a high percentage of The Body of Christ living joyless lives in a fantasy relationship with God because they haven't given themselves to spending intimate time with Him... becoming familiar and close to Him. I want to encourage you that spending quality time with Father God will be the BEST INVESTMENT you have ever made! SPEND THE TIME!

The Word of God says joy in Father's presence and peace to guard our hearts and minds belongs to every Believer. But what are we guarding our hearts from? From all the lies of the enemy that come to tear us down every time we experience hurt and/or rejection of any kind. If we receive them, these lies cause us to walk as weak, defeated people who are negative and have a consistent attitude of doom and gloom. And from that sad place we have a tendency to fantasize about "what could be" or "what could have been". The lies and thoughts of the enemy will always oppose who God's Word says we are and who Jesus gave His life for. The peace that passes our human understanding is the protective shield placed around our minds and hearts by Holy Spirit. It is a fruit of being intimate with Father God and allowing Him to touch the broken and hurting places of our hearts and minds. This peace is the fruit of our life that only grows because we are vulnerable and completely naked, and transparent in His presence.

Out of our intimate relationship, *trust* in the Lord grows as we hear His Word speak in our spirit. In Psalm 118:8, the Word of God says, *"It is better to trust in the Lord than to put confidence in man."* The word man in this scripture refers to *oneself as well as another*. Intimacy with Father God brings us to that place of trusting more in Him than even the confidence we have in our own thought and ability. As individuals and corporately, we MUST be the carriers of God's presence that has been birthed from our intimate time with Him. Fantasy requires our thoughts, will, and emotions to be fulfilled. Intimacy allows Father God to reveal Himself to us individually and brings the joy of the Lord, the protection of His peace, and reveals the true intent of His heart.

TRUST IN THE LORD

Life gets complicated at times, and some decisions that we must make force us to leave our theology (*the study of the nature of God and religious beliefs*) because it has not produced the answer and reconciled the issue being challenged. These times are some of the most stretching and pressing times for Believers because we are left with no option except to *"trust in the Lord with all of our heart and NOT lean to our understanding."* ~ Proverbs 3:5. These are times that can make us feel weak in spirit, soul, and body. Often when we look to our theology for the answer, we discover that our theology is simply a thought process we have adapted to and our issue demands a tangible resolve. When we give ourself to those sweet times of intimacy with Father God and we draw into Him, He will reveal *the truth* to us, which always supersedes our understanding. Sometimes we find ourselves in the place of decision when we must choose, my theology OR God's truth. At that very moment, our hearts beat and long for intimacy with the Father, not fantasy because we know that intimacy will bring the answer. Fantasy will only bring forth an idea of something that *could be*. The answer is ALWAYS to trust in the Lord, and out of trusting Him, truth is revealed, and the resolve comes.

In these moments, we should find ourselves saturating our spirits with thanksgiving, worship, and loving our Heavenly Father, becoming lost in the Word of God for hope, strength, and stability to bring sure and divine reconciliation to our situation. As we move through the minutiae of life, going to God's Word first and spending precious time alone with Him will allow the fragile places of our soul and heart to be ministered to from Holy Spirit. His transforming power is bringing us to the deep intimate place of *knowing* our Heavenly Father. Our honesty and transparency with Father God is the beginning of new life for us.

Believe me! There isn't any feeling, emotion, thought, word, or thing we've done that will cause Heavenly Father to fall from His throne. His desire to show Himself through His love for us is greater than all the ugliness that tries to hide in our hearts. God is faithful through His love, grace, and mercy to search us, expose us to ourselves, and make us aware of hidden yuck, so we are made aware of the healing we so desperately need. If our response to Father God in these moments is to *hear* what He is saying to us and *see* what He is showing us, we will receive the healing as Holy Spirit ministers life to us.

God does not practice spiritual birth control

JESUS IS THE HOLIEST OF HOLIES

Jesus has provided the way for us to live in the most glorious, intimate relationship with Father God if we willingly give ourselves and surrender our lives to Him. It is at the very moment of ***receiving*** His love and grace that we boldly enter that holy place with God. There is nothing more precious and treasured than knowing that I am in that secret place with my Father, where His presence is tangible and real. I'm reminded of the Old Testament high priest who went into the holiest of holies once a year for the atonement of sin and God would meet him in a cloud of His glory. What a privilege we are given because Jesus' death and resurrection have made it possible for us to *live* in that place every day! In our receiving His salvation, He has brought us into the most holy place to dwell and stand clean in the presence of God.

> *Hebrews 10:19-22 "Therefore, brethren, having boldness to enter the Holiest by the blood of Jesus, by a new and living way which He consecrated for us, through the veil, that is, His flesh, and having a High Priest over the house of God, let us draw near with a true heart in full assurance of faith, having our hearts sprinkled from an evil conscience and our bodies washed with pure water."*

Knowing how wonderful this is, I have to let you know that these times don't just happen by osmosis but by being intentional on our part. We must make time to be quiet and still to recognize who is in our midst and come into alignment with God's Spirit in us. Because of our salvation through Jesus, He already lives in us, Father, Son, and Holy Spirit, *ALL of HIM*. We have to bring our souls and bodies to a place of stillness so that our spirit man/woman is ministered to and made strong. These times of intimacy with Father God bring us to the awareness that we live according to the Spirit *FIRST* ...then soul and body.

When our spirit is healthy, our minds and bodies are healthy too. I think we forget that our spirit is the part of us that will live eternally. That's who we are! Does it not make sense that the part of us that will live eternally should live from the place of the Spirit's nurturing and leading? Jesus did when He was on the earth in flesh form. Jesus was intentional about spending time with the Father, and because He did, He was prepared to release life to the criminal on the cross even when He was in agony.

In the 21st century, society has become so busy with gadgets and systems created by man that we have become desensitized to intimacy and find it difficult to have alone time with our Heavenly Father. I personally believe that ***intentional intimacy*** should become the new buzz phrase for every born again believer. We must recognize our own need for those precious alone times with Father God because out of those times, we are made strong and resilient so when we face our own agony and adversity on the earth, we remain givers of God's love.

When we posture our heart towards Jesus and in our mind see ourself resting at His feet to receive from Heavenly Father intimately, He will redeem our lives in every area, restore strength to our souls and align our life according to His Spirit giving us a future of peace and hope.

Chapter 7

DO I SEE WHO JESUS SEES?

Much of our time on this earth is spent wanting to discover who we really are, who really accepts us, and where we fit in, and the truth is we should be spending our time discovering who God is. In our discovery of who He is, He reveals to us who we are. God desires that we respond to his wooing love for us whether we think we are worthy of it or not because He wants us to see ourselves the way He sees us. He has plans for us and has already executed his plan to reconcile us back to Himself through Jesus, our salvation because He is the one who KNOWS who we are!

Friend, do you understand the magnitude of what happened to each of us at our moment of salvation through Jesus Christ? It was more than just a price paid to keep us out of hell. The moment of salvation delivers us out of the darkness of sin and transports us into the light of God's Kingdom. We are ushered into God's divine order of living and prospering as His Spirit begins living in us. THAT IS REDEMPTION! *"He has delivered us from the power of darkness and conveyed us into the kingdom of the Son of His love, in whom we have redemption through His blood, the forgiveness of sins."* ~ Colossians 1:13-14. YES, Jesus paid the WHOLE price for our sick bodies, our ill feelings and emotions, our financial debt, our sin, our doubt and second guessing... EVERYTHING that would try and take us away from Abba Father. Salvation was given in every area of our lives because Jesus was reconciling us back to Himself. The discovery of God's thoughts and intent "for me" should be the top priority to every Believer.

You may ask yourself as I have, "Why would God do that for me?" And the answer is simple! Because He sees His creation in us, He sees us whole in our bodies, well in our minds, our spirits strong and at peace in the Lord. God transforms us into who He has created us to be, a new creature. Sometimes we do not see it initially and that is why trusting in the Lord is important to allow the transforming work of Holy Spirit in our lives. *"Therefore, if anyone is in Christ, he is a new creation; old things have passed away; behold, all things have become new."* ~ 2 Corinthians 5:17.

We discover who we are and why we are here through the process of transformation only if we allow the ministry of Holy Spirit. At the time of our salvation, the person we were in the sin nature no longer exists. That person has been made new by God's Spirit. Now we have to be reintroduced to ourselves through the Spirit of God to know who we are. Our own thoughts and our opinions have become obsolete, and now we are on a journey with our Heavenly Father to see and know ourselves through His eyes. Obviously, God KNOWS more about us than we know ourselves. God gives us GRACE as He demonstrates His love towards us even while we were sinners! *"But God demonstrates His own love toward us, in that while we were still sinners, Christ died for us."* ~ Romans 5:8. He did not wait for us to transform ourselves and *prove* ourselves worthy BEFORE He demonstrated perfect love. Father sees our value as His creation and understands that without the power of His Spirit to transform us, we would never be changed. We must receive the good and acceptable perfect will of God in our life through the transformation of His Spirit by the renewing of our mind.

As His Spirit lives in us, we transform with supernatural power, proving the perfect nature and will of God, our Heavenly Father. *"And do not be conformed to this world, but be transformed by the renewing of your mind, that you may prove what is that good and acceptable and perfect will of God."* ~ Romans 12:2. Father God wants us to receive the grace that transforms our lives to the point we show grace to others. When we can show grace to others, we are proving the good and acceptable perfect will of God.

As I said previously, our spirit is *reconciled* back to our Heavenly Father by grace at the moment of salvation, which we have believed in FAITH. The process of recognizing our true identity begins. Do not forget that we are spiritual beings who are having a temporary earthly experience, not earthly beings having a temporary spiritual experience. We have identified ourselves according to the natural elements, situation, and circumstances of our life and family history until salvation. As a Believer, we come into the spiritual dimension in life called the Kingdom of God, now identifying and defining our spiritual existence. We are no longer defined, identified, and bound by the natural. Now we are part of God's way of life and UNITY of His Spirit, and we must allow our minds to be renewed and reformed by His Spirit.

WE ARE CITIZENS OF THE KINGDOM OF GOD

Let me remind you, the man-made church system and ideas is natural because it was created according to man's interpretation of scripture and ideology of how we should conduct ourselves and gather as Christians. We have been called to live as sons and daughters of the King in His Kingdom....not members of a congregation. I am not saying we should all stop gathering, but I AM saying that we must allow the reforming of The Church to *align us SPIRITUALLY* to God's design, so we are worshiping in SPIRIT and TRUTH, not according to man's limited ideas and plans. *"God is Spirit, and those who worship Him* ***must worship in spirit and truth."*** ~ John 4:24. It is dangerous when Believers create boundaries that make them comfortable in worship, prayer, and bringing forth the Word of God because we take the risk of Father God not even recognizing our worship and

God did not wait
for us to transform
ourselves and prove
ourselves worthy before
He demonstrated
perfect love!

prayers. Many times He does not recognize what is being preached as His Word. GOD DOES NOT SEE US AS PART OF A MAN-MADE RELIGIOUS SYSTEM. HE RECOGNIZES US AS SONS AND DAUGHTERS OF HIS KINGDOM WHO ARE HIS CHURCH, THE ECCLESIA. Jesus said in Matthew 16:18, *"....And I also say to you that you are Peter, and on this rock **I will build My church**, and the gates of Hades shall not prevail against it."* The ONLY reason we have witnessed so much hell raging against our nation is because hell has raged against The Church. WE HAVE NOT ALLOWED JESUS TO BUILD HIS CHURCH! Jesus is the model of Kingdom boundaries for all Believers. He is the one who carries the blueprint of Father God's Church, and He understands what we look like. When Father God looks at His Church, He sees what HE HAS CREATED, not what we have made and brought forth from our own thinking, understanding, and interpretation. He sees HIS SPIRIT moving and molding all of us who will follow Him to be His Church.

"Therefore, my brethren, you also have become dead to the law through the body of Christ, that you may be married to another—to Him who was raised from the dead, that we should bear fruit to God." ~ Romans 7:4. We no longer are joined to *what was*, the old law covenant, but now have been brought into *what is* - **the new covenant of God's perfected love** ushered in by His grace and shown to us through Jesus Christ **bearing** His fruit. As His beloved who are married to Him, we are not to struggle, strive, or contend with life issues that will draw us away from Him. To really understand and receive the love of God through Christ Jesus, we must posture ourselves to receive continually from Him. We must throw out the notion that we can do anything or make anything work. In fact, we must accept that even in our weakness, God still sees us as His sons and daughters living *from* the place of victory! *"For we do not have a High Priest who cannot*

sympathize with our weaknesses, but was in all points tempted as we are, yet without sin." ~ Hebrews 4:15. When we allow Jesus to build His Church and be the strength in our relationship, the gates of hell will NOT prevail against us, and THAT IS VICTORY!

Our responsibility is to discipline our minds to remember that God sees us as he has created us for His purpose, and His Spirit living in us. He sees way beyond our natural ability, and understands the power of His Spirit in us, reconciling all things concerning our lives back to His design. We can only truly receive from Abba Father when we humble ourselves and admit that we need Him. In fact, Philippians 2:12 is often quoted by many religious people with a wrong understanding. It says, *"Therefore, my beloved, as you have always obeyed, not as in my presence only, but now much more in my absence, work out your own salvation with fear and trembling."* We have taught that we have the responsibility of *staying* saved through our good works and deeds. The last part of this scripture's true meaning is that we must work out who *has come to live on the inside us* when we receive Jesus Christ at salvation. The first part of that scripture is speaking of obeying, so we are working out or bringing forth the obedience to God's Spirit inside of us in every instance that salvation is needed, allowing Christ to come forth. We get ALL of Him at the very moment we are saved! Everything that was accomplished at the cross and resurrection becomes ours instantly. Still, we must work it from the inside to the outside with fear [*respect, recognition, and honor of God*] and trembling [*the distrust of one's own ability*]. We must humbly say that our personal ability is not enough to bring Christ forth, but we must yield to His power and allow Him to come forth through us.

We must fully understand we have NO ability in and of ourselves but MUST rely on God the Father, God the Son, and God the Holy Spirit to bring us to completion in Christ. We must be totally dependent upon HIM! That is how God truly sees us: incapable of absolute success and accomplishment without HIM because He has created us to dwell and abide in Him. We are God's sons and daughters, and He loves us from that reference point. My question to all of us is, "Do we respond as a son or daughter to Him?" We can correctly respond when we understand and accept how we are related to God.

HE CALLS ME HIS OWN

In Luke 15, we read the story of the prodigal son. We do not know the family's name, but so that I can make this point, let us just call them the Smith family. Let us say the son's name is John. When John left home with his inheritance, his name was still John Smith. As he was spending all the inheritance having fun and living frivolously, his name was still John Smith. When he found himself broke and in a country suffering famine, he hired himself out to feed the pigs, and guess what! He was STILL identified as John Smith, the name which his father gave him! His circumstances and the desperation of his immediate situation did not change his name or identity to his father; he was still John Smith. I want us all to remember right now that whatever we may be going through, even if it is of our own making, God STILL identifies us as His sons and daughters. If our Heavenly Father still calls us his own, we should too, and not allow our perspective of who we are in Christ to change.

When John Smith came to the end of himself and his own ability, he returned to his father, hoping to be received even if he had to offer himself as a servant. The Bible says that even before he made it to the house, his father saw him coming down the road from a distance and ran to meet him. His father put his arms around his neck and began to kiss him; BEFORE the son said he was sorry! The dad saw *his son*, not a man who had made bad choices and squandered everything he had been given. That is a perfect picture of love and redemption.

Our Heavenly Father sees his sons and daughters, not people of bad choices and failure. He has run down our road of self-inflicted pain and hard consequence to wrap His arms of love around us, kiss us with goodness, and redeem us!

We are all on a journey of self-discovery to truly understand who our Heavenly Father sees and calls us. Through Holy Spirit, He is constantly wooing us to Himself so that our perspective will come into alignment with who He knows us to be. He is the one who knows His plans and purpose for each one of us.

RELATIONSHIP TRUMPS NAME

When my boys were little, I remember a time that the youngest one Nicolas came in one evening with his friend as I was cooking dinner and asked a question. "Mom, can my friend eat dinner with us?" I replied, "Well, of course, Nic! What's your friend's name?" Nicolas had his arm around his friend's neck and looked at him as he said, "Hey, what's your name?"

I LOVE that Nicolas only recognized the friendship and relationship, as new as it was, and it did not matter that he knew his name. Too many of us get caught up in *needing to know* the name, description, title, plans, etc. that Father God has for us before entering that precious *relationship* with Christ that brings us into the truth of who we really are. Through our relationship with Father God, our true purpose is unveiled, and we recognize that we are the reflection of Jesus. His love penetrates our natural cell walls to bring forth supernatural life in our spirit man/woman, and Jesus is brought forth. We can see in the life of Jesus that relationship with people was most important to Him. He wanted them to feel His love for them, healing their hearts and bringing reformation to their life. He always saw people through eyes of love and compassion, *knowing* that what He brought them would change their lives forever and align them with Heavenly Father and His Kingdom.

In Song of Solomon 4:7, the scripture says, *"You are all fair, my love, and there is* ***no spot in you****."* Ephesians 5:25-27 *says, "Husbands, love your wives,* ***just as Christ also loved the church*** *and gave Himself for her, that* ***He might sanctify and cleanse her with the washing of water by the word****, that He might present her to Himself a glorious church,* ***not having spot or wrinkle or***

We are spiritual beings who are having a temporary earthly experience, not earthly beings having a temporary spiritual experience.

***any such thing**, but that she should be holy and without blemish."* We are fooling ourselves if we think God does not know the truth of who we are. He sees our reality like no one else can or ever will, and He also sees the finished work Jesus Christ has provided for us to sanctify and cleanse us so we can live as His bride, holy and without blemish. He wants us to see we are sons and daughters of the King, we are righteous because of Jesus, we are well and whole, living fulfilled and complete in Him.

The Father desires that we will see ourselves as He sees us, unleashed in this earth with unlimited possibilities to bring the fulfillment of His Kingdom to reality NOW! I do not know about you, but I cannot answer honestly and say that I have always seen myself in this way. I am actually a work in progress. I can say that I am beginning to discipline myself to speak these words over my life to remind myself that who God sees and loves is what matters, not what my circumstances say or what I say about myself.

RELATIONSHIP WITH HIS WORD

Circumstances and reality are not necessarily the truth. Here is what I mean. A Believer could receive a bad report of a disease or sickness from the doctor, which is the reality of the moment. But, the truth is that they are well and whole according to the Word of God. *"who Himself bore our sins in His own body on the tree, that we, having died to sins, might live for righteousness—**by whose stripes you were healed.**"* ~ 1 Peter 2:24. Your reality right now could be that you have a child who has run away and "disowned" you as their parent, but as a Believer, that is NOT your truth! Your truth is, ***"And he will turn the hearts of***

the fathers to the children, And the hearts of the children to their fathers.... *"* ~ Malachi 4:6 and *"**And he arose and came to his father**. But when he was still a great way off, his father saw him and had compassion, and ran and fell on his neck and kissed him."* ~ Luke 15:20. Or maybe your pantry is bare, the gas tank is empty, and your bank account is overdrawn, making for a desperate reality but remember that is not your truth! The truth is, ***"And my God shall supply all*** *your need according to His riches in glory by Christ Jesus."* ~ Philippians 4:19. As born-again Believers, we must not say what is against the truth of what God says about us! His Word of truth always lets us know how He sees us, and it will always win over the part of our reality and circumstances that are not in alignment with His Spirit. But we must accept and receive what His Word says concerning us. Our relationship with Father God and His Word is our insight to know who we are and the truth of our life. When we choose to believe His truth in the midst of our reality we allow God to override unfavorable circumstances and situations as His Word brings life and restoration every time!

To really understand who I am as God sees me requires me to listen to Him, or in other words, I must let His words concerning me be louder than what I say to myself. I must disarm all my defenses, excuses, and justifications to receive the Word promises that God has given me to walk in. If I respond positively to God's view of me being bigger than my mind can conceive but I struggle to *believe* His Word concerning me, how can I make the shift? Just *realizing* that what God says about me and who He sees is bigger than my own mind can conceive pushes me to humbly **accept** and **believe** in **faith** what God has spoken is the truth about ME. The more I read His Word and allow Holy Spirit to speak to my heart, the more He penetrates the shell of protection I have created and replaces it with His peace that guards and protects my heart. As I accept His truth about me, I begin to see a glimpse of the daughter that my Heavenly Father loves so deeply.

Chapter 8

HOW I SEE MYSELF SAYS HOW I SEE YOU

Believe it or not, my life and yours are not for our own benefit and control or to be turned inward after being born again through Christ Jesus. Our life's purpose is to equip and fortify others as we move and live in the abundant love of God through our daily interactions with each other. If my life was my own, I would be of no use to anyone else, and I would only be something to *watch* on social media. To some individuals, that is their desire. They are sentencing themselves to a life of emptiness, void of joy because they have totally missed the sound of God's wooing them into His intimate love relationship with them.

When Believers can understand the significance and strength of God's Spirit of love inside of us, our vision and perspective of others begins to take on a whole new level of accountability and crushes our own formed, often times, misguided opinions. No longer can I see others through the filter of my thoughts, judgments, and criticisms that are all limited and have been formed or based on my own prejudices, mood, or feelings. In the same way that I allow Holy Spirit to bring clarity of who I am and whose I am, I must be willing to see others the same way. As I am in Christ now, I must ask myself, "Is my opinion of *you* in alignment with God's opinion and thoughts of me? Remember, in the previous chapter, we discovered that our identity never changes to God, and His love for us remains unconditional even through bad circumstances, bad opinions, and bad choices we may have made. He continues to identify us as His sons and daughters, and because He lives in us, we must give the same response to others. As Christ lives through me, I must allow His vision of you to be my vision of you. I can only see you as I see myself when I look upon Him.

If we are Christ in the earth now, the way we identify others must remain in the same perfected love that we have received, remember God's love transcends all of *our* opinions and thoughts of ourselves and others. For me to truly see you as God sees you, I'm required to set Godly boundaries around my thinking and opinions. I set the boundaries concerning myself first, by testing every thought and opinion I have about myself against what the Word of God says. Are my thoughts about me in alignment with what God says about me? When I believe what His Word says concerning me, I can see you as He does. For a lot of people, they see the negative about others because they see the same negative in themselves. But if we can come to the place of seeing ourselves correctly, according to the Word of God, we will find it easier to see and love others the way Christ does. If I have received His grace and what He says about me, do I give His grace to you and speak what He says about you?

*"1 Peter 4:10 As each one has received a gift, **minister it to one another**, as good stewards of the manifold **grace** of God." ~*

REVIVAL TO REFORM

As I find myself lost in the love of God and the character of Jesus continues to take form in me, I realize that there is more time spent blessing others and receiving them as they are rather than trying to correct everything that doesn't measure up to my opinion. When our spiritual leadership, collectively, receives the same revelation of Father's love and presence to bring forth Jesus' character, I believe we will see *unity* as we have never witnessed before. We will desire to gather together beyond lines of social status, denomination, membership, race, and culture

When I believe what His Word says concerning me, I can see you as He does.

that have kept us divided. When we begin to see each one as sons and daughters of Father, our brothers and sisters of the Kingdom of God, *revival* will truly have begun in the hearts of individuals. This personal revival will usher in God's *reformation* of His Church in our nation and around the world.

> *Ephesians 4:1-3 "I, therefore, the prisoner of the Lord, beseech you to walk worthy of the calling with which you were called, with all lowliness and gentleness, with longsuffering, bearing with one another in love, endeavoring to keep the unity of the Spirit in the bond of peace."*

We will witness The Church making every effort to keep the Unity of Holy Spirit by being peace-*full.*

It is time to mature in our thinking and be real with our thoughts and answer the question, "why do I have the opinion I have concerning this person or that one?" Especially as leaders, if we would truly be honest with ourselves, I think we could agree that too often we have made choices and decisions out of offense and fear of what *could be* or *might happen* if we allow Holy Spirit to have His way of Unity. We have even tried to silence anyone who we have considered to be outside of our *circle*. Instead of TRUSTING that God is speaking to others just as loudly as He is speaking to us, many have believed the lie that they are the only ones Father speaks to concerning the whole Body. Many choose to call their circle a special kind of covenant that excludes all those who disagree. My beloved friend, I cannot find anywhere in the New Testament that we are to enter into covenant with only those who think like us, act like us, and agree with everything we believe. I do not find any scripture to support the idea that God even recognizes our covenants we have entered with one another. No, the only covenant I have been able to find is the one of Jesus' unconditional love that has the power to annihilate all lines of division. As we enter that covenant with *Him*, then we recognize all the others who have entered the same covenant in the same way. Entering *His* covenant [marriage to Jesus] comes with a command from Jesus, *"And you shall love the Lord your God with all your heart, with all your soul, with all your mind, and with all your strength.' This is the first commandment. And the second, like it, is this: You shall love your neighbor as yourself.' There is no other commandment greater than these."* ~ Mark 12:30-31. The commandment of Jesus will ALWAYS trump the covenants we have entered with man.

The man-made church system and covenants are birthed out of an agreement of theology and ideas, which is no commandment of Christ. He says that we must simply love Him with all our heart, with all our soul, and with all our mind and love others as we love ourselves. In that commandment alone, we fulfill the whole law because Jesus fulfilled the law through love; He is God's manifested love.

> *Matthew 5:17 "Do not think that I came to destroy the Law or the Prophets. I did not come to destroy but to fulfill."*

The heart desire of our Heavenly Father is that we would all live in unity with each other through His love. It is quite simple, loving each other because He has loved us, this is the Father's desire for all people because He loves all people. When we receive His love, he pulls us into Himself, and we become the tangible extension of His love here on the earth.

LET'S BE REAL

The demand for authenticity could not be greater than it is right now in the days we live where the magic of makeup, camera filters, website design, clothes, auto-tune, etc. make it possible for us to paint any image of ourselves that we desire. Authenticity can become hidden if we do not keep watch and guard our mind and heart. The very definition of authentic means *original and real*. The truth of God is authentic and real, and it will always come forth to make an impact in the world. Authenticity will always shine brighter than a self-created image *trying to paint a picture* of truth. When we allow God to show us who He is in us and how He has created us to be unique in this world, we begin to find that the shoes of authenticity are comfortable to walk in. I constantly ask myself, "Who am I without makeup and filters, away from the pulpit, away from the website and

Being authentic is essential for us to be able to see others as God sees them.

social media, and without my best high heels on? Would I still be able to impact a hurting soul with the unique gifts that God has given me? Am I able to identify God's greatness in others? Do I accept others in the same love and compassion as Jesus? Does my gift function without all the extras like false eyelashes, fake nails, and self-tanner? Would I still be able to bring love to the unloved, and would I be able to draw on the truth of God's Word because I know what it says? "

If I come to a place that I can't answer *yes*, that is the indicator that I must go to my Heavenly Father and receive His love and grace to heal me in that particular area and allow Him to guide me through His Word to the truth. When I feel insecure or unmerited, I must allow His love to transcend all my thoughts and opinions to bring me back to His thoughts and truth concerning me. When I have heard people's opinions that have brought me low, it is my responsibility to remind myself that God has brought me high, and in Him alone, do I excel and find that He is effective through me to the hurting. Nothing can bring you lower than hearing the hurtful criticism and judgmental opinions of your peers. In these times, I would encourage everyone to find out who they truly are as sons and daughters of our Heavenly Father so that they are nothing but authentic in their presentation of the love and gospel truth of Jesus Christ. Authenticity can penetrate the hardest of hearts and minds because others will *feel* and *experience* the love of God through it.

Being authentic is essential for us to be able to see others as God sees them. When we are authentic and true to our own uniqueness in God, we are confident because of His Spirit in us, and the need to be *the best there ever was*, and the need to be *front and center* is erased. We move in boldness and assurance that God is the one working through us, and He gets all the glory because I have died to self and become *the least there ever was* knowing that His strength is made perfect in my weakness. It is easy for me if others only see Jesus through me and never know my name.

> *2 Corinthians 12:9 "And He said to me, "My grace is sufficient for you, for My strength is made perfect in weakness."*

When I know that, I can see others the way He shows me, with His unconditional love and grace poured out even if their character and lifestyle is the polar opposite of mine. I WANT others to see the strength of Jesus in me so they know they can draw from the same source and be strong and confident too.

Jesus was the most authentic person to ever live and walk on the earth. Because He has the same heart as God the Father, he could walk with no judgment or criticism towards others. He was confident because He walked on the earth knowing that He is God in the flesh, and HE IS THE ANSWER TO EVERYONE'S LIFE ISSUES. I understand that it can be mind-blowing to think the same about ourselves, but that is the beautiful truth of why Holy Spirit has come to live inside us. As we submit to Holy Spirit, allowing Him to transform us and follow His leading, we will move according to the heart's desire of our Heavenly Father toward others and walk with the same confidence and revelation that we are Jesus with skin on in the 21st century. We will walk in all assurance that God is bringing His answer to fruition through our obedience to Him. We are just vessels to pour out His Spirit to others.

I know many struggle with even the word *authenticity* because they do not understand who they truly are. We live in a world that is so drawn to believe that only the big moments and events in life make up a person's true identity, and that is a lie. We measure God's effectiveness through our life on the earth by the popularity we have or do not have with people. Even running to Facebook to check the likes and comments has become the measure for many to determine how effective they are in Christ. DO NOT GET CAUGHT IN THAT TRAP!! IT WILL CAUSE YOU TO LOSE SIGHT OF WHO GOD HAS CREATED YOU TO BE, AND YOU WILL NOT ACCEPT YOUR UNIQUENESS!

On my journey to understanding authenticity, I had to look truthfully at myself to discover the qualities and uniqueness that God has placed in me and be ok with what they are. Even if I do not look like someone else or have their same qualities, If I am not the most popular on social media, I must know *that I know that I know* that God did not miss the mark when He created me! I must have the assurance and confidence that who He created me to be is perfection in Him.

I asked the Lord to let me see who He sees when He looks at me, and it made the process a lot easier than me trying to discover who I am on my own. He showed me how I am an encourager to people, genuinely wanting them to reach their God-given potential. I will walk in love with them through the issue of life they may struggle with and continually point them in the direction of Jesus. I am a happy person who always sees the cup half full, and I am optimistic in every negative situation. I rejoice every day - when I feel at my best and when I am not - knowing that God is still mighty and strong even in that very moment for ME! His Word even declares that He is working everything for my good.

> *Romans 8:28 "And we know that all things work together for good to those who love God, to those who are the called according to His purpose."*

He let me see how I trust Him and easily take Him at His Word; I do not struggle to believe Him. I trust that He has my best interest at heart, and He is faithfully moving on my behalf to bring His full purpose for my life to fruition.

I take His word seriously as though He has written it specifically to me. I truly desire to love freely and give His love and grace without hesitation because that is how He has given Himself to me. I want others to see Christ in me and allow Him to do a work of restoration in their own soul renewing the thoughts they have of themselves to align with what Father says about them. Being authentic is not hard when we allow Christ to do all the work. Authenticity is simply allowing God to bring out what is on the inside of us. If we would just allow Him to come forth, He will use us as His vessel to transform the lives of those He connects us with. Authenticity works from the inside to the outside, not the other way around. I discovered a long time ago that it takes less effort to be real and honest with people through the filter of God's unconditional love than it does to maintain an image based on my own opinion and criticisms of the world around me. The question I ask daily, probably more than any other question, is simple: Where would Jesus be standing in this situation if He were still in flesh form on the earth? That perspective, my friend, has the power to change a lot of our own thinking, and it may even help us respond to situations and circumstances in a way that will bring resolve and healing into the matter.

As we walk together along this earth journey, know that I am looking at you through the lens of revelation that Holy Spirit has shown me about me. I am listening to Him as He whispers His thoughts to me. Settle back for a moment, get comfortable, and be still. Allow Father God to whisper to you all the wonderful truth of who He has created you to be. Let Him remind you how uniquely and wonderfully He has made you, nothing neglected or forgotten, but all things made perfect in Him.

Being authentic is not hard when we allow Christ to do all the work.

Chapter 9

THE 1 FACTOR

1 John 4:17 says, *"Love has been perfected among us in this: that we may have boldness in the day of judgment; because* ***as He is, so are we in this world****."* "SO ARE WE" is a strong statement, but it is the truth of who God created us to be...ONE with Christ His son! This means that we are as He is NOW, RESURRECTED AND RIGHTEOUS, all things alive and well. His NOW must become our NOW to live in the fullness of His presence. The possibility of this truth being manifested demands that we move out of the way and allow Christ to live His life through us.

The number *1* is unique as it can only be divided by itself, and even then, it remains 1, and it cannot be divided by any other number. It is a whole number and is the first number that begins all other whole numbers: 1, 2, 3, 4, 5, etc. It can only be added to and never taken away from by another whole number. Whole numbers are positive numbers. If you can visualize a number line, 0 being in the middle and whole positive numbers to the right and negative numbers to the left, you will notice that 0 has no positive value until we add the number 1, 0+1=1, now 0 has a value. The numbers to the left of 0 reflect the negative value, or no value of the positive whole number to the right of 0. Is it not true that the enemy always tries to turn our sight on the negative value of who we are? That is why we must understand the importance of the greatest number 1 in our life, our Heavenly Father. Nothing can divide Him; He stands alone with *whole* value. Nothing I do or say will ever be able to cause Him to come apart and divide from who He is, God the Father, God the Son, and God the Holy Spirit. Deuteronomy 6:4 says, *"Hear, O Israel: The Lord our God,* ***the Lord is one!****"*

God is the 1-FACTOR in my life that does not come apart under pressure or difficulty because He IS WHOLE! He existed long before the foundation of the earth was formed, and we were created in the atmosphere of His infinite existence. If my life is a 0, and I add God, I have added value to my existence. The more I allow Him to manifest and be fruitful in my life, the more of His "completeness" I become. Father God knows everything about me and how He created me, and He knows the same about you. Before we allow Christ to save us and bring us into an intimate relationship with our Heavenly Father, we find ourselves always looking at the left side of the number line of our life, and all we see is a negative value. But because God is **unity**, **order**, and **alignment, the 1-2-3** of His will and purpose for our lives, the only way we can bring ourselves to the place of positive life value is to yield and surrender our heart to Father God. He is the first *whole* with value, and we must be in unity with Him.

God is the 1-Factor in my life that does not come apart under pressure or difficulty because
He IS WHOLE!

We could all save ourselves some heartache and needless frustration by simply allowing Holy Spirit to take us by the hand and walk us right to God's perfect plan, but unfortunately, more times than not, we make it hard for ourselves. Many of us struggle because we constantly focus on the wrong side of 0 in our lives. In God, even when we feel like a 0 with no value, we can become whole with positive life value! It is somewhat daunting that God would choose to empower us with His Spirit on the earth. But, that is what He did when He sent Jesus, His only son, first so that we could experience His love and compassion from an earth perspective. When we receive the gift of salvation through His son Jesus Christ, we have taken our first step in the process of becoming one with Him. I have heard many say throughout my years of ministry and travels, and I have even said it myself, "I'm one with Christ!" However, I never considered wholeheartedly what that exactly meant.

HOW TO GET FROM -1 TO 1

There is a voice in the earth teaching that God helps those who help themselves, which is simply not true. God helps those who *allow* Him to help them because they have lost themselves and literally come undone. Those who have surrendered their thoughts and will to Him and rendered themselves dead to self are alive in Christ, alive ONLY because they have received the full work of the cross and ALLOWED Christ's resurrection of their life. God can fulfill His Kingdom desire and design for us to be effective in the earth when He is the only one, 1, standing. When I allow God to be that 1-FACTOR in my life, I become all that He intended me to be, and my life is complete through His love and favor. *"I have been crucified with Christ; it is no longer I who live, but Christ lives in me; and the life which I now live in the flesh I live by faith in the Son of God, who loved me and gave Himself for me."* ~ Galatians 2:20.

God's design has always been that we live in unity with His Spirit. According to His Word, that requires us to allow Holy Spirit to reconcile everything back to Himself, which instructs us to *endeavor (strive) to keep* the unity. (I will speak on this in the next chapter.) *"I, therefore, the prisoner of the Lord, beseech you to walk worthy of the calling with which you were called, with all lowliness and gentleness, with longsuffering, bearing with one another in love,* ***endeavoring*** *to keep the unity of the Spirit in the bond of peace. There is one body and one Spirit, just as you were called in one hope of your calling…."* ~ Ephesians 4:1-4. Before we can even begin to entertain the thought of living in unity with each other, we must be in unity within ourselves to God, Jesus, and Holy Spirit. We are made up of a spirit, a soul, and a body. Our spirit will live eternally and is where God lives. Our soul is our thoughts, will, and emotions, and our body is the earth suit that holds it all together. Our body will respond to either our spirit or our soul, and whatever we feed our spirit and soul is who we become. Much of the time, our flesh is screaming and fighting to have what it wants according to our own thoughts, will, and emotions. Whether it is good or bad for us, we will justify having it and devise a plan to have it through our own thoughts. This always leads to plotting, scheming, and manipulation to ensure that we get what we want. If you are one who struggles with this very behavior, I suggest that you may be spending too much time looking at the wrong side of 0 on your number line. Begin to look at the whole value of 1 and add yourself to Him.

The Bible is clear about sowing to our flesh and feeding our desires; it all leads to corruption. *"For he who sows to his flesh will of the flesh reap corruption, but he who sows to the Spirit will of the Spirit reap everlasting life."* ~ Galatians 6:8. God's design for all of us is that we live according to His Spirit and be led by His Spirit because He truly wants us to be whole and prosperous in our life. *"Beloved, I pray that you may prosper in all things and be in health, just as your soul prospers."* ~ 3 John 1:2. Only He knows what His Spirit is bringing forth in His good time to fulfill His purpose and who *we are* for that purpose. We must allow Holy Spirit to show us who we truly are, and that may take us beyond our own understanding of who we *think* we are. Jesus gives us the blueprint to who we are and the life we live on the earth as Believers. In His life, He allows us to see his thoughts, will, and emotions that not only bring the answer but brings forth the character of Father God.

We are His treasure and His vessel to bring forth His goodness in the earth. "*But we have this treasure in earthen vessels, that the excellence of the power may be of God and not of us."* ~ 2 Corinthians 4:7. We must bring our flesh into the control of God's Spirit and *trust Him* and know that when we do, we are sowing to the Spirit of God who brings forth His Kingdom through our lives. Our spirit must yield to the Spirit of God and allow Him to have our mind. *"….but be transformed by the renewing of your mind, that you may prove what is that good and acceptable and perfect will of God."* ~ Romans 12:2. Our body (our actions) will align with either our spirit or our soul, which one are you feeding? Our thoughts, will, and emotions will determine the outcome of our lives. It IS possible for our soul to be in unity with the Spirit of God…to think as He thinks, speak like He speaks, and do His will as Jesus did. The 1-FACTOR, the one who can stand alone, is God who *is* LOVE and who came to earth in the form of man, Jesus. Jesus came in LOVE to be love; He was love in spirit, soul, and body. In other words, He moved from His Spirit, which is love, making His thoughts love, His will love, and His emotions love. His body actions were always love and compassion, bringing all who would receive Him into the wholeness of Father God. That is Kingdom life in Christ.

*We will never know
true righteousness, peace,
and joy until we know
the love of God.*

THE KINGDOM OF 1 IS LOVE

God desires that we flow from His Kingdom that was created in us before we were even born. Jesus said in Luke 17:21, *"...For indeed, the kingdom of God* ***is within you****."* In fact, the message of Jesus from the very beginning of His ministry is that the Kingdom of His Father is NOW!

> *Matthew 4:17 "From that time Jesus began to preach and to say, "Repent, for the kingdom of heaven is at hand.*

For all of us, we must learn what Jesus meant in His message of Kingdom. In the book of Romans, Paul spells it out for us in chapter 14, verse 17, *"For the kingdom of God is not eating and drinking, but* ***righteousness and peace and joy in the Holy Spirit.****"* We will never know true righteousness, peace, and joy until we know the love of God. We are living in times that are revealing a huge part of the Body of Christ has an attitude that says, "What's the big deal? I love God, and He loves me. His grace has covered me, and that's enough".

This is true but skewed at the same time because it is not simply a matter of the love connection between God and us, and Jesus shows us that. He shows us how far God's love will go when we live from His Kingdom that is within us. We are created to live from the righteousness of God, the peace of God, and the joy of God through His Spirit. Our standard is to be *right by God* and bring His peace and joy into all we are called to do. Let me take this a little further for you, so you understand how important our standard is. If you have ever watched movies about Kingdoms up to about the 17th century, you will see that when the army of the Kingdom arrives at the ground for battle, the officers on horses carrying the flags that identify the Kingdom go first. Those flags are called the *standard* of the Kingdom. In Isaiah 59:19, we read, *"....when the enemy comes in like a flood, The Spirit of the Lord will lift up a* ***standard*** *against him."* The Hebrew meaning of the word standard in this scripture means *display; to flee; to take flight*. As Believers, if we have allowed Jesus' own identity to be our identity, our standard is a message to the enemy that we belong to God, and we have the power and authority to tell him to flee and take flight away from us. When we position ourselves behind God's standard, in other words, when we allow God to come forth first as number 1, He announces and displays His authority to defeat the enemy in our lives and win the battle over our struggles. When we allow Holy Spirit to move our negative thoughts and emotions to the positive side of our number line, we become whole with the number 1, and we have a new standard. Now, being whole, we can *be* righteousness (right by God), and peace and joy extended to others from His Kingdom inside us. Sometimes loving others the way Christ has loved us is simply responding to them the way Jesus responds to us. The *whole* fruit of God's Kingdom love is given through the actions of peace and joy towards others. The banner of God's Kingdom is love.

> *Song of Solomon 2:4 "He brought me to the banqueting house, and* ***His banner over me is love."***

The Hebrew meaning of the word banner in this scripture means *STANDARD*! Oh, how I hope you are beginning to see who you truly are and the Kingdom that is inside you, THE KINGDOM OF LOVE! God rules His Kingdom in love, and we are citizens of love, so righteousness, peace, and joy are who we are, and our work is righteous. We are not working to be righteous, but our work or action is righteousness.

> *Isaiah 32:17 "The work of righteousness will be peace, and the effect of righteousness, quietness, and assurance forever."*

When we truly join ourselves to number 1, others become our focus ~ not ourselves. As we mature and grow in the nature of God's love and His Kingdom ways, we become unarmed of our defenses and simply carry the love of Jesus everywhere we go. We will find that we live much happier lives when our attention is set on discovering how we can be our best and bring our best to help someone else fulfill God's calling in their life.

When we are faced with difficult circumstances, we can push through with all assurance that righteousness and peace are ours, and we can draw strength from knowing that the 1-Factor in life is all-consuming and secure. Because we know with all certainty that Father God has our lives in His control, and He is moving on our behalf for our good, we can set our attention and concern on helping and ministering to others. Jesus is the one who God sent into the earth, wearing an earth suit, allowing us to see, feel, hear, smell, and taste His love to understand who He is. Psalm 34:8 says, *"Oh, taste and see that the Lord is good."* God desires that we allow Christ to continue to live in the earth through us so that others will know that the Lord is good.

We will never be able to convince people of the Lord's goodness with our mere words. When we find ourselves on the right side of 0 on the number line of life, we align with Father God, and our spirit person is walking with Holy Spirit revealing our wholeness, and they will *see* the goodness of God. Our life will speak louder than our words. We all need to ask ourselves: "Am I drawing from who I know Christ is living in me, and have I allowed His love and compassion to minister to me in the areas

The more we allow God's love to add value to our lives, the more we want to add value to others.

of my life where I see the negative and no value?" If the answer is *no*, that is a clear indicator to get back into alignment behind God's Kingdom standard because His love supersedes all the negative and brings wholeness to my life. We will all find out that the more we allow God's love to add value to our life, the more we want to add value to others.

I recognize the need for me to be in unity with the 1-Factor. My earth journey demands that in the same way Jesus was one with the Father while He was in the earth, I must receive *all of Him to be one with Him.* Others will only be saved and know the love of God as they are in unity with the 1-Factor who can stand alone; His name is love.

Chapter 10

FROM THE 1 FACTOR TO 1 FAMILY

Ephesians 4:1-6 says, *"I, therefore, the prisoner of the Lord, beseech you to walk worthy of the calling with which you were called, with all lowliness and gentleness, with longsuffering,* ***bearing with one another in love, endeavoring to keep*** *the unity of the Spirit* ***in the bond of peace.*** *There is one body and one Spirit, just as you were called in one hope of your calling; one Lord, one faith, one baptism; one God and Father of all, who is above all, and through all, and in you all."*

Also, look at Romans 15:5, which says, *"Now may the God of patience [endurance] and comfort* ***grant you to be like-minded toward one another, according to Christ Jesus, that you may with one mind and one mouth*** *glorify the God and Father of our Lord Jesus Christ."*

I believe that in these two scriptures, Paul paints a beautiful picture of how we are to live and walk together as one body. He instructs us to *keep* the unity of the Spirit, which means it already exists, and we are to watch over it and protect it. In our *bearing with one another in love*, we are *keeping* the Unity of the Spirit, *who is* our bond of peace. Everywhere we look in scripture, we can see love is the glue that holds everything together in this life because it is the foundation of who we are Spiritually. Did you catch that? Our life on earth is held together because of who we are **Spiritually**.

As we have individually come into unity with Jesus Christ, we have come into Unity with the Body of Christ. I think many in the Body of Christ do not understand that they are in unity with each other, whether they like them or not lol. There seems to be a wrong understanding in the Body of Christ that we are trying to *get into* unity instead of accepting the truth that *we are already in* Unity, and we must KEEP it! Sadly, when we look at the Body of Christ, we are not seeing what God has said in His Word concerning one mind and one mouth of His Unity. Instead of endeavoring to keep the Unity of God's design, we have allowed the Body of Christ to be divided by denomination, race, social status, culture, and many times by simply being offended by someone. We have found others who think and speak as we do (those who have the same convictions we have), and then, we go to work to make OUR way THE way. We draft a list of beliefs and bylaws according to what we determine is right and wrong. Many races have their own culture, and within the culture, there is a social *climb* that is looked upon and valued as the measure for success in the man-made system we have called "Church." Culture and social status are two main factors that have the power to determine our thought process in life, and out of that, many denominations are born of man. We have even allowed division among us through being offended by disagreement. If we as Believers are not careful to surrender these things to

Holy Spirit individually, we will not live in the truth of unity by keeping our unity to Father God, Jesus, and Holy Spirit. We may find ourselves standing alone, simply doing our own thing.

As we look at The Body of Christ now, she is BROKEN AND SICK! She needs to heal. We must allow Holy Spirit to do His perfect work in us, ALL of us.

> *Romans 12:4 & 5 "For as we have many members in one body, but all the members do not have the same function, so we, being many, are one body in Christ, and* ***individually members of one another.***"

> *1 Corinthians 12:27 "Now you are the body of Christ, and members individually."*

Paul is specific in describing her to us; we are 1 FAMILY ~ ONE BODY, yet many members. And just like in our human body, our arms, legs, and head are attached. Our eyes, nose, and mouth are on the front of our face, and our ears are on the side of our heads. Looking at the Body of Christ now, there are arms and legs everywhere, and noses, mouths, ears, and eyes are scattered all over. Trust me, Jesus is coming back for His *whole and healthy* Bride, who is ONE BODY WITH ALL MEMBERS ATTACHED. Paul even says that we are individually members of one another. YIKES! That means that you are part of me, and I am part of you whether I like you or not and whether you like me or not. Lord God, HELP US! The Body of Christ suffers from a spiritual autoimmune disease; the Body has turned on herself and is attacking her own members. She is in poor condition because we have allowed her to move closer to human ways of thinking and understanding influenced by the world. Further from the supernatural Kingdom ways influenced by the very Spirit of God. Unity is so important to God that where He finds it, He commands His blessing upon it.

> *Psalm 133 "Behold, how good and how pleasant it is* ***for brethren to dwell together in unity!*** *It is like the precious oil upon the head, running down on the beard, the beard of Aaron, running down on the edge of his garments. It is like the dew of Hermon, descending upon the mountains of Zion;* ***For there the Lord commanded the blessing— Life forevermore.****"*

Now, I am not a scholar by any means, but I am smart enough to know if the Word of God says it is good and pleasant for us to dwell together in unity and God commands the blessing of life FOREVERMORE in that place, I must take responsibility to do my part so the Body of Christ can heal.

THE COST

We have not insisted that the Unity of Holy Spirit be protected at all costs, even if the cost is our own will. When we demand our way, we are opposed to receiving love from Father God and giving love to others. Here is the perfect picture of love:

> *"Love suffers long and is kind; love does not envy; love does not parade itself, is not puffed up;* ***does not behave rudely, does not seek its own****, is not provoked,* ***thinks no evil****; does not rejoice in iniquity, but rejoices in the truth; bears all things, believes all things, hopes all things, endures all things." (1 Corinthians 13:4-7)*

Paul tells us in Ephesians 4 (see above) to bear with one another *in love*, and the manifestation of that is laying down my life. I become a bridge for others to walk across if they need to, helping them get to the other side of their issue. Oh, did you hear me? Bearing with another means it will cost me *my* life because it requires me to lay down my way, desire, and opinion and not think evil of them, but I believe and hope the best for them. I can only lay my life down when I have received the *love life of Jesus* to resurrect in me.

Throughout the Body of Christ, we have allowed the spirits of judgment, criticism, pride of self, and greed to be the hierarchy of our denominations, race, social standing, and culture. We have even allowed our behavior to be club/cult-like as the Mason's with a *secret handshake*. Those who know the secret handshake can come in, but if you don't, you will not be welcomed until you are indoctrinated into the belief system and agree with what has been determined by men to be the order of the club/cult. We have even tried to own the word *covenant* as though it belongs to our group and/or us. The word covenant is

The Body of Christ suffers from a spiritual autoimmune disease; the Body has turned on herself and is attacking her own members!

Jesus' word describing His love and way into the Body of Christ; it has nothing to do with our own select group.

> *Hebrews 9:15 "And for this reason He is the Mediator of the* ***new covenant, by means of death****, for the redemption of the transgressions under the first covenant, that those who are called may receive the promise of the eternal inheritance."*

I have to ask myself, and so do you, "am I willing to die to my own way, my own thinking, and my own feelings to be in the covenant of perfected love? We enter into covenant with Jesus Christ, our brother, vertically, taking our rightful place as a member of the Body of Christ. Man does NOT get to make that determination or qualify us. Instituting horizontal covenants within the Church is a dangerous move because God is left out when a "man" hierarchy is set in place for governing AND horizontal covenants bring division within the Body of Christ. Horizontal covenants are self-serving, and the vertical covenant of love is Kingdom serving. I learned a personal lesson about horizontal covenants in 2014 when I experienced, for the first time, a group of leaders tell me I was no longer in covenant with them. I won't go into detail because I don't want to expose anyone or bring the same hurt and rejection to them that Marla and I experienced as a ministry team. But I DO want to bring exposure to the lie that so many of us have bought into, and that is the one of believing that we can actually enter horizontal covenants with each other. Even the true marriage covenant between a man and a woman is vertical and includes God the Father. God has brought them together as they have each been in a relationship with Him first, and the same is true for the Body of Christ to be revealed. We must all be in a love relationship with Father God individually, and in doing so, we will find **all** the other members of the Body of Christ, and the ***whole*** will be seen.

KEEP WHAT IS OURS

We're not called to be in covenant with each other; we are called to KEEP the UNITY of the Body of Christ! WE ARE A BODY, THE PERSON JESUS CHRIST!

> *Ephesians 4:1-6 "I, therefore, the prisoner of the Lord, beseech you to walk worthy of the calling with which you were called, with all lowliness and gentleness, with longsuffering, bearing with one another in love,* ***endeavoring to keep the unity of the Spirit in the bond of peace. There is one body*** *and one Spirit, just as you were called in one hope of your calling; one Lord, one faith, one baptism; one God and Father of all, who is above all, and through all, and in you all."*

As Christians, we have often focused on issues that are not heaven or hell issues; we have even tried to play Holy Spirit and police the behaviors of Believers only to break unity by bringing division. All we were instructed by Jesus to do is to love each other and bear with them. Listen, when Holy Spirit profoundly changes someone, their transformation does NOT require that we police them and judge them according to what they do or do not do. We are to walk with them in the love of Christ and build them up with the Word of God, NOT tear them down by reminding them of their sin or be the mediator between them and the Father during their process.

The man-made church system, the machine, in no way resembles the Kingdom modeled by Jesus and His disciples in the earth, one Body joined together and held together by God's love. Maybe it will help you to see it this way: "the Kingdom of God is an *organism* that grows from *a relationship* with Father God, and the man-made church system is an organization formed by man." ~ Paul Radke III.

I have said it previously, but I will say it again, God does not need our programs, big buildings, big platforms with lights and smoke to be effective in getting His message of love across. All of those things are good to create a temporary experience that touches the soul of those present but does not guarantee that someone will have an eternal spiritual encounter with Father God. The Church must have an everlasting encounter with Father and not settle for an experience that will fade away. For the message of God's love to be heard, we must be willing to protect our Unity and go forth to *be* love to others. We may not have all the "bells and whistles," but trust me, they are not required! If you do not believe me, test my words. Go beyond your four walls and find someone who is truly hurting and down and out; then, love them. Go beyond just giving them something to eat or a bottle of water; spend quality time with them, listen to them, and let them know they are being heard. Allow them to speak from their reality of hurt, disappointment, or brokenness, and be God's love to them. His love is the total absence of judgment, criticism, manipulation, scheming, threats, and control. His love is not intimidating but welcoming and accepting. I have never known anyone to refuse real love, and I guarantee you that when you leave, they will say that there is something different about you, and maybe that they felt something they never felt before. As we have surrendered our life to Heavenly Father and continue to yield our way to Holy Spirit, He comes forth from our life and touches the heart of others.

It grieves my heart to see how empty of Christ so many of the spiritual leadership and so many shepherds of God's people have become. Many are self-absorbed and extravagant in their own opinion of themselves and have managed to make themselves untouchable. I call it "celebrity-itis." I wonder if they even hear Holy Spirit as He whispers to them or even recognize opportunities that God Himself has orchestrated to bring all of His gifts (the apostle, prophet, evangelist, teacher, and pastor) into His Church as a whole. Some leaders now do not hear God because their own thoughts and board members are the loudest voices they hear. Many are trying to build an empire, hoping to succeed in notoriety and wealth. It grieves me too that instead of being humbled enough to allow Holy Spirit to do what He desires through them, they would rather plan the next big conference or schedule themselves to be out and about away from the sheep they have been charged to watch over. Though The Church in the 21st century is deficient in so many areas, God is healing us and making us **whole as He sees us!**

REFORMATION HAS BEGUN

God is raising His Kingdom apostles and prophets who truly love His people to bring His order in the Body of Christ, teaching and encouraging us to keep unity with Father God and each other. Those who model His design of living life together in the love of Jesus Christ and protecting it are beginning to emerge as forerunners full of mercy and grace through the love of Jesus Christ. His love is bringing us back into alignment so that we keep and protect our Unity according to His Word. There is such expectation in the Body of Christ right now to see revival. Revival IS HERE because the hearts of the people are sincerely turning to God. Father is revealing Himself to us in ways we have never known Him before, and we are finding Him right in the middle of our own personal issues! When we seek His face and desire His will above our own, we find Him every time we are faced with circumstances beyond our control. We *know* revival when we protect our Unity with God the Father, God the Son, and God the Holy Spirit in our personal life first. As we are revived individually, *reformation* will come to the Church.

Before the COVID-19 Pandemic, many were having what they called "great moves of God" in their houses of worship, but they chose to remain divided. I question if God birthed the move, or if man created an emotional atmosphere and experience for Christians. I question because God is UNITY, and we are ONE BODY, not divided. As we have lived through mandated lockdowns and restrictions placed on our corporate gatherings, we are seeing what God has birthed through Holy Spirit because the fruit of His love is emerging in a beautiful way. Members of the Body are speaking out and sharing in their homes and on social media Father's love and His Word. We are witnessing the sheep themselves being the encourager, teacher, and evangelist. True worship is transcending the false need for big sound systems, lights, words on a giant screen, and a full band to be effective. It is a beautiful testimony to us that God will have His way and Jesus is taking back HIS CHURCH!

When we are genuinely walking in love, we are concerned about keeping Unity because we are all *members of one body, the Body of Christ.* When we keep Unity, we will see denomination go away. Leaders will stop self-promoting and self-appointing, and we will witness them outwardly loving each other regardless of title or position. We will see a mind shift in our leadership as they realize their very life is a platform to bring the message of God's love and His Kingdom. They will realize that a pulpit, congregation and weekly scheduled time are not the requirements, boundaries, or driving force of God's present tangible love. The spiritual bullies will stop bullying other Believers, and the self-righteous will fall to their faces in humility and cry out to Father God. Even as I write this now, many are being challenged because they have been forced to find alternate ways to bring forth the message of God's Kingdom and His love. There are restrictions on our corporate gatherings right now which may possibly limit us to only be able to gather with the ones in our homes. But I am encouraged because I see that even the natural limitations have not stopped us from being The Church and bringing forth the love of Jesus. Unity does not require everyone to be in the same building within the same four walls. Unity is being revealed in the Spirit as God is bringing us together spiritually. We are Spirit to Spirit with Him and He is bringing us together; it is BEAUTIFUL to see how we are effective as we move in the love of God that we have received. God's Kingdom order is being established, and our way does not seem to be as important anymore. The numbers in pews and the tithes' records are no longer a priority as *total trust and dependence on Father God* is returning to our leadership. The confidence that came from hearing the praises and validation of people, the favor of the board, and the *business of doing church* is being replaced with a life of faith, keeping leadership in constant communication with Heavenly Father.

There is a remnant that is allowing God to raise them up to reach out at ALL costs to bring truth and healing to the Body of Christ. He is bringing forth leaders who are teaching the truth in the love of God, not being motivated by self. As leaders, we **must allow Holy Spirit to do a work of healing and mending**

The keepers of the unity of the Spirit of God are the reformers of The Church.

of the broken places of our heart so that we can trust our Heavenly Father and live in faith, *believing* all that God's Word says about who we are. We must initiate the healing process by humbling ourselves and truly repenting of our own way and thoughts. We must take away all the mechanisms that we have created to guard our hearts and let Jesus have it in the purest way. You will know you have successfully done that when you feel completely naked and vulnerable. Only when we open our hearts to Jesus will we be positioned to receive the powerful, unfailing, transforming love of our Father God.

As we no longer disengage but engage in our beautiful love relationship with Jesus, Holy Spirit emerges in our speech so that we are **speaking life** from God's Word no matter the circumstance or situation. Because we are receiving, we are being saturated in the love of God and the righteousness of Jesus, peace is our message, and joy is our attitude. Keeping and protecting the Unity of the Family of God requires me to lose all judgment and criticism of all members. Yes, even when God will use some as iron to sharpen me! I must trust that Holy Spirit is the same in them as He is in me even when I focus on their qualities or shortcomings, forgetting that I must only focus on Jesus Christ. Remember vertical first, and then horizontal.

When we look to people for acceptance and validation, we can often feel rejection because the expectation we have placed on them is greater than they can deliver. None of us is created to fill the void in others, whatever it may be. When we feel let down or rejected by others, we become defensive and build walls that keep others out because we believe the pain is too intense to live through again. I have felt rejection at different times in my life as a wife, as a friend, as a sibling, and as a leader in the Body of Christ. I have experienced the pain and heartache of not being heard or accepted, and though the pain is real, praise Jesus, it is NOT eternal! If Holy Spirit can bring me into His supernatural alignment, He can do the same in others. When I humble myself, Holy Spirit gently disarms me from all of my defenses that have kept me from knowing the precious and valued side of a relationship with those who have hurt me. There is always value in relationship with others because God has created us all, and He intends that we dwell together in unity through His love.

I have a visual right now of a child who has found a shotgun and is totally unaware of how dangerous it is and how much devastation and destruction it can bring. I see a loving father slowly walking up to the child and gently taking it out of their hand. The Father knows the destructive nature of our defenses that we bury in our hearts better than we do, and He wants to disarm us and free our hands to praise Him and embrace each other. I must remain conscious of the beautiful work that His love is doing in me and doing in them. It is my responsibility to guard my heart by drawing into Father's presence and listening to His voice so that it is louder than the hurtful words of rejection. It is my responsibility to bring the reconciling love of Jesus Christ in everything I do.

> *Proverbs 4:23 "Above all else, **guard your heart, for everything you do flows from it.**"*

KEEPING UNITY IS REFORMATION

I can no longer entertain thoughts of negativity about my brothers and sisters, opinions that allow rejection and offense to enter. By the way, negative opinions are the doorways that allow all forms of ugliness to enter our hearts. I must not ignore Father God's desire that I love others and bear with them when they are hurting and needing to be restored.

> *Colossians 3:13 "bearing with one another, and forgiving one another, if anyone has a complaint against another; even as Christ forgave you, so you also must do."*

> *Ephesians 4:2 "....with all lowliness and gentleness, with longsuffering, bearing with one another in love...."*

I desire to see others the way Father God sees us all: with purpose and value, accepted because of Jesus' love for us. Someone else's restoration is just as important as mine, and I must take the time and be available and desire to be a part of their process, whatever that may look like. Jesus says in Matthew 10:42, *"And whoever gives one of these little ones **only a cup of cold***

water in the name of a disciple [of Jesus Christ], assuredly, I say to you, he shall by no means lose his reward." The measure or *size* of our help may be small in nature, but when given with the heart of Father's love, it always comes with reward not only to the one we are helping but especially to our life.

Gone are the days of allowing our own thoughts, emotions, and will to dictate our journey. God is moving among His people right now, bringing all things into His order. He is bringing forth His Kingdom Family in the earth, and we are keeping the Unity of the Family. Only God knows what is on the horizon for each of us to accomplish our purpose in His big picture. We cannot even fathom His thoughts and ways concerning us.

> *Isaiah 55:9 "For as the heavens are higher than the earth, So are My ways higher than your ways, And My thoughts than your thoughts."*

Because we do not know, we must press into Him daily for instructions and guidance from Holy Spirit so we are not ruled by our own thoughts and emotions. At this very moment, God is calling everyone in the Body of Christ to do what they need to do to protect and keep our Unity in His love. We are stronger when we stand together, undivided as 1-FAMILY, determined to see our Father's will established on the earth.

Each of us has a beautiful purpose to fulfill in the grand scope of all that God is doing and it is His delight to move through us to see that accomplished. Our responsibility is to bring our fighting, kicking, and screaming flesh to the altar of God's love every day and lay it down. In laying down my life, I can be assured that God will move by His Spirit through me to resurrect His life through me to those around me. As I endeavor to keep the Unity of the Spirit in the bond of peace and protect the Body of Christ, God's family, I am bringing reformation to

The Church. **THE KEEPERS OF THE UNITY OF THE SPIRIT OF GOD ARE THE REFORMERS OF THE CHURCH.**

To all my Brothers and Sisters ~ I bless you to live intentionally in an intimate relationship with Heavenly Father. I bless YOU with all love, grace, and mercy from Jesus. I declare that in this season, in your NOW, you will see the salvation of the Lord in all the areas of your life that you know yourself to be helpless, hopeless, and needing a love intervention of Father God. I bless you to allow God to penetrate the hardest places of your heart and purge you with His healing love through compassion. I declare that you will hear His song as He rejoices and sings over you.

> *Zephaniah 3:17 "The Lord your God in your midst, The Mighty One, will save; He will rejoice over you with gladness, He will quiet you with His love,* ***He will rejoice over you with singing****."*

You are positioned to be the best YOU in the earth because of the greatness that God has created in you. I bless you to walk in the love of Jesus as you have received the full measure of His love in your own life. I bless you as you allow Holy Spirit to transform and renew your mind and bring all your thoughts into His Holy alignment according to God's Word. I bless you in these days of process as you begin to see your vision full of hope and desire, as you move away from self and into God through His love and His Word. I bless you to declare over your own life the same Words of life that all of Heaven is speaking over you. I bless you to protect the Unity of our Family as God has called us to live in His love and love one another because **we are** the Body of Christ, the Bride for whom Jesus is returning, and we are beautiful!

www.ingramcontent.com/pod-product-compliance
Lightning Source LLC
LaVergne TN
LVHW020628100826
845148LV00012B/2096

* 9 7 8 0 9 5 6 7 2 7 7 9 4 *